WALKING FAST

WALKING FAST

Therese Iknoian

Human Kinetics

Library of Congress Cataloging-in-Publication Data

Iknoian, Therese, 1957-
    Walking fast / Therese Iknoian.
        p.   cm.
    Includes bibliographical references (p. 169) and index.
    ISBN 0-88011-661-7
    1. Fitness walking. 2. Walking (Sports)   I. Title.
    GV502.I45   1998
    613.7'176–dc21   97-38947
                                                                        CIP

ISBN: 0-88011-661-7

Permission notices for material reprinted in this book from other sources can be found on page xiii.

Developmental Editor: Marni Basic; **Assistant Editor**: Henry V. Woolsey; **Copyeditor**: Jim Burns; **Proofreader**: Erin Cler; **Indexer**: Prottsman Indexing; **Graphic Designer**: Nancy Rasmus; **Graphic Artist**: Angela K. Snyder; **Photo Editor**: Boyd LaFoon; **Cover Designer**: Jack Davis; **Photographer (cover)**: © Tony Stone Images/Brian Bailey; **Photographer (interior)**: Ken Lee, except where noted; **Illustrators**: Paul To and Joe Bellis; **Printer**: United Graphics

Human Kinetics books are available at special discounts for bulk purchase. Special editions or book excerpts can also be created to specification. For details, contact the Special Sales Manager at Human Kinetics.

Printed in the United States of America   10   9   8   7   6   5   4   3   2   1

Human Kinetics
Web site: http://www.humankinetics.com/

United States: Human Kinetics
P.O. Box 5076
Champaign, IL 61825-5076
1-800-747-4457
e-mail: humank@hkusa.com

*Canada:*Human Kinetics, Box 24040
Windsor, ON N8Y 4Y9
1-800-465-7301 (in Canada only)
e-mail: humank@hkcanada.com

Europe: Human Kinetics, P.O. Box IW14
Leeds LS16 6TR, United Kingdom
(44) 1132 781708
e-mail: humank@hkeurope.com

Australia: Human Kinetics
57A Price Avenue
Lower Mitcham, South Australia 5062
(088) 277 1555
e-mail: humank@hkaustralia.com

New Zealand: Human Kinetics
P.O. Box 105-231, Auckland 1
(09) 523 3462
e-mail: humank@hknewz.com

*To my mother and father, Roxy and Richard, for being an unfaltering,
two-person cheerleading squad through all the ups and downs,
and for always believing I'd make the right choices.*

*And to Michael, for daring to take that leap into the future,
and for showing me the true depth of a trusting, honest,
and loving relationship.*

CONTENTS

PREFACE

I took the back door into walking, not unlike other devout walkers you will meet.

Motivation to stay fit with less impact is what attracted me initially. In my teens and through college, I was a dance maniac, gravitating to studios to take jazz and modern several times a week. That led to taking aerobics after college graduation. Knowing I was headed to Europe for school, however, I needed a convenient and accessible form of fitness. Aerobics studios were going to be rare. So I "taught" myself to run. As the books advise, I started with 10 minutes, slowly increasing to about 30 to 40 minutes after a few months. Never did I know how fast I ran. I just ran.

About 5 years later, after my return to the United States, my knees started to speak to me—just little twinges—and I quit frequent runs, turning primarily to health clubs and teaching aerobics for fitness. I'd heard about walking and its great fitness benefits, so I tried it. Although it felt good, I just couldn't reach the rates of sweat and breathing that I knew and loved from other workouts—until I read about race walking and tried the technique. I studied pictures in magazines and experimented with the style along the beaches in Monterey, California. I was immediately sold on fast walking, devoted myself to learning more, and began trying to convince other fitness professionals, such as aerobics teachers and personal trainers, and their students that they too could get a workout from a walk.

Alas, I wasn't always successful. You see, that was unfortunately in the mid-1980s, before most of the public was willing to accept a low-impact workout as good enough, or walking as a real sport or viable fitness activity. I plugged along, preaching the truth of walking every chance I got, often only to small audiences and people who thought a window-shopping pace was brisk. Not one to give up easily, I would bet runners and other very fit people who pooh-poohed walking that if they went for a walk with me they would indeed get a workout. I saw more than a few eyes open wide after a few minutes.

Now, there's nothing wrong with slow to moderate walking. Studies show that health benefits are substantial, and I'll encourage any person to do something at any pace rather than nothing at no pace. But preaching a pleasant walk for health is a different topic for a different audience. This book is taking the next step for those who are ready for it.

With no training I was immediately able to do an 11-minute mile (which dropped considerably with training), so it was natural for me to break out of that box of just fast walking for higher fitness and to try racing. I found racing and formal training gave some focus to my program. Instead of just working out every day for the goal of, well, working out, I was working out with a goal of doing well in an event next week, next month, or next year. I was challenging myself with every workout and charting gains of time, distance, and endurance.

Race walking, too, is where I met what I call my extended family— a network of people around the country who understand the joys and occasional frustrations of training and racing at all levels. In nearly any city where I travel for business or pleasure, there are fellow walkers I can call without hesitation for walking information, best routes, club camaraderie, or just a friendly meal. Once you're bitten by the competitive bug, whatever your level, it's difficult to back off. For one, your walking friends won't let you and, two, your quest for personal records, or PRs, is never-ending.

I find it a continual source of entertainment that people you pass on a trail think that it's appropriate for runners to go fast, but that walkers should go slow. "It's OK. No one's behind you. You can slow down," I've been told a few times. Or people just ask why bother walking if you're going to go fast; why not just run, comes the question. Well, I say, sometimes you feel like playing volleyball and sometimes you feel like playing basketball. They are both ball sports, but very different, and you wouldn't settle for one when you prefer to do the other, would you? Same with running and walking. Both involve moving in a straight line on both feet, but they are very different, and you wouldn't do one when you like the other better. Walking, you see, is not slow running.

Personally, I choose to see the world mainly while gliding through a walk, not bouncing along in a run. I prefer to improve my fitness while also challenging my physical and mental ability to master a special technique. I like doing something fast that also feels like a graceful dance.

You too can fast walk and be fit.

ACKNOWLEDGMENTS

A raft of sports and science professionals lent their ears and expertise as I began in this book to formalize walking workouts and training programs—matching, sorting, puzzling over, and cross-checking the science of running, the science of training, the smattering of research on walking and race walking, and the art behind all of that. Many thanks go to Ron Daniel, past national race walk champion and international judge, for consulting with me on the menu of workouts and programs, as well as reviewing other bits and pieces along the way. He was able to draw on decades of walking experience as a coach and racer. I'm also grateful to Dr. Jack Daniels, renowned running coach, researcher, and an all-around down-to-earth guy, for taking a few moments from his busy schedule to review training physiology as I'd applied it to walking. Appreciation also is given to Dr. Betty Wenz, one of the founders of sport psychology as we know it today, who unwittingly taught me many lessons about dealing with workouts, athletes, life, and the art of balanced training—lessons I have tried to convey in this book. Drs. Cal Caplan and Cathy Inouye served on my master's degree committee, and I thank them for the great support and patience they gave me, as well as for the information they provided me, during the years I spent completing my degree in exercise physiology.

Also, I feel inclined to think back on the journalism teachers who had a great impact on my becoming a writer: Carole Sarkisian, my high school teacher who always thought I should go into journalism when I thought it sounded hilarious at best; Tom Johnson, who gave me a D on my first writing assignment as a college sophomore, serving to fire me up and challenge me to show him better (his intent, I now know); and Betty Medsger, who gently convinced students they were worth something and who always supported my choices. Many thanks to all.

And what about my walking family? I can't begin to name them all, but sincerest gratitude to the legions of novice walkers I have taught and cheered on over the years; to the race walkers—especially the Golden Gate Race Walkers and others in the Pacific Association—who believed in me when I raced and whose questions partly spurred me on to formalize this book; to the top-ranked walkers I have watched and admired; to the best friends I've made among walkers around the country; and, certainly, to the kids I've coached, who have rewarded me with one of the purest joys I have ever experienced.

Great appreciation also goes to the race walkers of the Pacific Association who volunteered to be technique models: Ron Daniel, Diane Fitzpatrick, Nik Sakelarious, Kim Wilkinson, and Sandy Womack.

My family, too, has given incredible support, encouraging writing, walking, and traveling projects even when they didn't quite understand what it all meant. None of this would be possible without them.

To all I say, keep your feet moving.

CREDITS

Figure 3.1 adapted, by permission, from A. Hreljac, 1993, "Preferred energetically optimal gait transition speed in human locomotion," *Medicine and science in sports and exercise* 25: 1158-1162.

Figures 3.17, 8.1, and 8.5 adapted, by permission, from USA Track & Field, 1996, *Race walk judging handbook* (Indianapolis: USATF), pages 9, 9, and 8 respectively.

Figure 6.3 adapted, by permission, from D.E. Martin and P.N. Coe, 1991, *Training distance runners* (Champaign, IL: Leisure Press), 133.

Table 2.1 adapted, by permission, from American College of Sports Medicine, 1995, *ACSM's guidelines for exercise testing and prescription* (Baltimore: Williams and Wilkins), 18; and from *The journal of the American medical association* 269: 3015-3023, 1993.

Table 4.1 adapted, by permission, from J.H. Wilmore and D.L. Costill, 1994, *Physiology of sport and exercise* (Champaign, IL: Human Kinetics Publishers, Inc.), 233.

Table 4.4 reprinted, by permission, from G. Borg, 1982, Rating of perceived exertion (RPE) scale. In *Psychophysical judgment and the process of perception*, ed. H-G Gessler and P. Petzold (New York: Elsevier). Reprint requests to Professor G. Borg, University of Stockholm, S-106 91 Stockholm, Sweden.

Table 4.5 adapted, by permission, from T. Iknoian, 1995, *Fitness walking* (Champaign, IL: Human Kinetics Publishers, Inc.), 53.

CHAPTER 1

FAST WALKING, FAST RESULTS

When you walk, you walk. This is serious performance because you want maximum results. But a question begins to tug at a corner of your brain: "Is there more?"

There is. Whether you walk every day, several times a week, or as serious cross-training, you can indeed step up your exercise intensity, fitness level, and performance.

Mastering the next step that will help you reach your goals only takes knowing more about two things: technique and training. I will cover both in this book.

In terms of technique, walking isn't just slow running. Learning a little about the biomechanics of fast walking and why it helps to move certain ways will give your performance and fitness a tremendous boost.

In terms of training, walking faster and getting more fit doesn't mean striding as fast as possible on every walk. Whether you are a fitness walker, a novice race walker, or a fitness enthusiast who wants to walk more, knowing what different types of workouts will do for your body, how to adapt the workouts to your schedule, how to combine them for safe and effective performance, and when to rest can help you take great strides toward your goals.

When you see the term "race walker," don't shy away if you don't want to race. Race walking is just an advanced form of walking technique that requires participants—if they compete in judged races—to comply with rules. Race walkers come in all shapes, sizes, and speeds. Many never even race, but might adapt the technique to their own powerful fitness walking. You too can enjoy the increase in cardiovascular and muscular benefits that come from race walking and, if you prefer, never worry about being judged.

Simply put, some of you will borrow race walking technique to apply to your fast fitness walking. Once you are bitten with the fast walking bug, however, you might decide to dabble at a few just-for-fun races, or you'll learn to better appreciate the efforts of those Olympic and national-class race walkers who are "just walking"—even though they're going faster than many of us can run!

Others will take the rules and racing tips seriously. Interestingly, many top-level race walkers started as fitness walkers who simply wanted, as you do, to step up their exercise intensity and fitness. A frequent member of the national race walking team, Kim Wilkinson of Monterey, California, was "discovered" striding quickly through a park by a local race walker who suggested she refine her technique and compete. Master race walker Phyllis Hansen from New Jersey was a runner-turned-walker who could soon stride so quickly she sought more than brisk fitness walks around the town.

Recognize, then, your reasons for walking faster and know that I will satisfy all of these as you progress through the book's details about technique and training. Some of your reasons might include meeting a personal challenge to walk faster, seeing if you're interested in racing, making the next step into race walking competitions, finding a satisfying alternative to running, or even meeting people through the international social fraternity of walking. Your secondary reasons might include achieving greater gains in health such as lower cholesterol and blood pressure, losing additional weight by using more calories, increasing aerobic fitness, or shaping leg and hip muscles.

WHAT DO YOU CALL YOUR WALKING?

Perhaps you've noticed that I've referred to walking by several names. You're probably familiar with other names too: speed walking, Olympic walking, performance walking, aerobic walking, brisk walking. I've had people ask what the difference is. Acquaintances and students

© New England Stock/Kristen Olenick

have asked how they can power walk or what the difference is between fitness walking and aerobic walking. With hundreds of names for walking—many conjured up by modern entrepreneurs looking for a way to identify themselves and register trademarks in the hope of increasing visibility and profit—it can be confusing.

Walking is walking. That's it. You might go faster, or you might go slower, but if you're putting one foot in front of the other for your health, fitness, or performance, you're walking. Forget the fancy names and trying to classify one area of technique as approved for a particular type of walking and not for another. Good technique applies to all speeds and labels.

Forget trying to decide if you should power walk, athletic walk, dynamic walk, or health walk. Just walk. Fast. With good technique. I only use different names for variety, although some names express variations. For example, fast or speed walking means moving more quickly than usual, as the adjectives "fast" and "speed" express, but there are no rules about how fast you must go before you are officially fast walking. What's fast for one person might be slow for another. If you've picked up this book, you're interested in walking faster, which might mean managing 13-minute miles or hitting sub-8-minute miles. Fast is relative.

There is one exception to this walking-is-walking rule: race walking, which is also known as Olympic walking because it's an Olympic event. Be forewarned that it is never known as power walking; those who race walk consider that term an affront and simply call it "walking." Race walking is merely an advanced walking technique. Note that you don't have to race to race walk, nor do you have to travel with the speed of light to race walk. Just applying the technique of rolling hips, strong arm swing, and fluid leg-and-knee action can classify you as a race walker and help you derive more muscular benefits and move more smoothly. There are two rules to race walking, but if you don't compete in formal, judged race walks, you don't even have to worry about those fine details. Just use what you need to find the performance and fitness you seek.

STEPS TO HIGHER PERFORMANCE

As you progress through the book and we dig into the fine points of good technique and training, you'll learn details about how to get more from your workout. Although there are other good fitness walking books, miscellaneous well-done endurance and running training books, and a smattering of decent race walking books, none of these has tried to bridge the gap between basic fitness walking and advanced race walking with quite the scientific approach presented here. You'll find science—physiology, biomechanics, and kinesiology—broken down for everyday consumption and understanding.

Look for information about:

- **Getting started**—Take a good look at your present speed and technique, and take a moment to assess your walking experience and goals.

- **Technique**—Achieve the most efficient arm swing, pushoff, stride length, and—if you're interested—the race walker's marked hip movement to help you accomplish your performance goals. Look for a list of common mistakes, ways you might determine if you fall prey to them, and how to fix them so you can develop the most efficient style.

- **Walking workouts**—Look for a breakdown of different zones and their physiologic principles, why you'd want to bother with each, how to apply them to your routine, and how to measure them using heart rate and perceived exertion. We'll give you samples of each kind of workout—for example, aerobic capacity, anaerobic threshold, and anaerobic capacity—in formal and less structured formats for you to use and modify to fit your individual plan.

- **Training programs**—Combine the different workouts in a performance and conditioning program, be it relatively unstructured, or more highly structured (for example, one that requires track work and more exact distance measurement and timing). Do not miss the information about how to make sure you don't become overtrained and how to keep your body healthy. Again, look for sample programs.

- **Challenges of racing**—Against yourself, against the clock, or against others, a race can fire you up and push you to new heights. We'll cover casual road races, as well as brief you on the technicalities of formal race walking, where to go for more information, and how to tap into the national network. This will be a primer on formal race walking rules, judging, and competitions.

- **Keeping track and staying motivated**—Logging workouts is an important tool at many levels and helps with motivation.

By the early '90s, attitudes about walking as a sport and true fitness activity began to evolve. Maybe that's why you're walking and interested in reaching higher levels of performance.

Know that you are participating in one of the oldest Olympic sports. Take pride in that because you, as a walker, are an athlete!

Chapter 2

Paving the Path to Performance

My assumption is that if you've picked up this book you're not a beginning exerciser. Either you are a regular brisk walker, a fitness enthusiast, or you participate or compete at some level in another sport.

Still, taking the time for a few basic assessments will help you establish a safe and effective walking program that will not only keep you injury free, but will also allow you to progress more steadily toward your performance goals.

Assess Your Health

Before you go any further, it's important to make sure you are healthy enough to continue with a more advanced fitness program like fast walking. Even if you've been active for a while, you might want to take a look at the following medical screenings. The first, to assess readiness to begin activity, is a health check-up to screen for latent high risks that might mean trouble. Most of you will glance at, visually check off with a string of "no's," and move on. But don't give this initial screening too short a shrift. Read each question thoroughly, especially if you've never looked at any other health screenings before.

HEALTH CHECK-UP

Fast walking can be a strenuous physical activity. Answer the questions in the box below before starting this, or any other, exercise program.

If you answer yes to any of the following questions, you should see a doctor for the go-ahead before you start a training program. If you answer no to all questions, increase your walking program gradually, but see a doctor if any answer changes to yes.

	YES	NO
1. Are you inactive now?	___	___
2. Do you smoke?	___	___
3. Do you have any history of heart disease or chest pains?	___	___
4. Did a brother, sister, mother, or father have heart disease before age 50?	___	___
5. Do you have high blood pressure, diabetes, or high blood sugar?	___	___
6. Do you have any joint problems, such as achiness or stiffness, that are worse when you exercise?	___	___
7. Are you taking medication for high blood pressure, diabetes, high blood cholesterol, or any other medication that might change your physical response to exercise?	___	___

Also, don't take too lightly the guidelines by the American College of Sports Medicine for those who plan to participate in a more organized or vigorous program. Taking a look at your risk factors is an important part of stepping up an exercise routine. Many of us have always been healthy, but might still have a predisposition for coronary heart disease because of age or gender. Look at the risk factors presented in table 2.1. If you're reading this book, risk factor 7 shouldn't apply.

If no more than one factor from table 2.1 applies to you and you seem to be healthy and have no symptoms such as those in the health check-

Table 2.1 ACSM Risk Factors

Positive risk factors	When
1. Age	Men older than 45 or women older than 55 or having had premature menopause without estrogen therapy.
2. Family history	Father or other immediate male family member who had a heart attack or sudden death before age 55; mother or other immediate female family member who died before age 65.
3. Cigarette smoking	Current smoker.
4. High blood pressure	Blood pressure of 140/90 or greater on at least two separate occasions; on medications for high blood pressure.
5. High blood cholesterol	Total cholesterol greater than 200 or HDL less than 35.
6. Diabetes	Insulin dependent and older than 30; insulin dependent for more than 15 years; or non-insulin-dependent diabetes and are older than 35.
7. Physically inactive	No regular exercise or recreation and a sedentary job.

Adapted from ACSM 1995 and JAMA 1993.

up, then you should be able to continue safely. If you have two or more of the risk factors or have any of the symptoms, you could be at increased risk. It would be best to see a doctor for medical clearance before increasing your intensity. Anyone with known cardiac, pulmonary, or metabolic diseases must receive a physician's clearance for safety.

ASSESS YOUR WALKING SPEED

Before beginning, take a couple of sessions to assess how fast you now walk for two distances—1 mile and a quarter mile—not worrying about technique. You will use these speeds not only to help you plan the speeds of workouts, but also to assess your progress. For example, you could retake these assessments every 6 to 8 weeks to help track your fitness gains. If you have a wireless heart rate monitor, wear it in both tests and track your heart rate throughout. Also, remember to warm up properly before any intense effort such as these assessments.

1-MILE WALK

On an accurately measured course, walk 1 mile as fast as you can, making sure you start and finish strongly. For exact measurement, if possible choose the first lane of a 440-yard school track and walk four laps. If this is not possible, use a distance-marked recreation trail or measure a mile with your car. (If you use a 400-meter track, you will have to walk four laps plus 9 meters for 1 mile.) If you're wearing a heart rate monitor, glance at it twice during a lap to mentally note your pulse. Notice if it climbs to a certain point, then stabilizes, since this will be a good indication of training speeds for you to apply later. If you don't have a monitor, take your heart rate for 15 seconds immediately after you stop and multiply by four to find your beats per minute.

1-Mile walking time	_____
Heart rate at finish	_____

Your peak heart rate as you finish, matched with your total time, will give you an indication of how soon you'll be able to walk longer workouts as you begin training.

QUARTER-MILE SPRINT

Again, choose an accurate course such as a quarter-mile school track, a paved trail marked for distance, or a section of street you've driven for distance. If possible, have someone else time you. Since this starts and ends so quickly and you'll be so out of breath, pushing buttons on a chronograph watch might be difficult. Walk all-out the entire distance. Note (or take) your heart rate and log your speed.

Quarter-mile sprint time	_____
Heart rate at finish	_____

This should be a fun, adrenaline-filled kick. Plus, you'll be able to plan sprint workouts later based on the speed ability you've demonstrated. I have distinct memories of the first time someone challenged me to walk a quarter mile all out. I'd been walking for a couple of months, but never so short, never so fast, and never timed. I tried to hedge my way out of it, but he wouldn't let up. So I plunked myself down at the starting line on a track. He yelled, "Go!" and I flew, having no idea how fast I was going. By 250 yards, I thought my lungs were going to blow. Coming into the home stretch, I recall looking down that long straightaway ahead and thinking, "I can't finish this." But my competitive juices—although only against myself—were flowing. I finished with a 2-minute lap (an 8-minute mile pace). That was it! I was hooked!

That little sprint boosted my confidence in my latent speed ability, prompted me into more structured training, and led me into fruitful years of competition and fun. It can do the same for you.

AGE-GRADING

Another way to assess how your 1-mile pace compares to other walkers of all ages around the world is to use tables (table 2.2) prepared by the World Association of Veteran Athletes. If your age is between two ages listed, split the difference in time for a good estimate.

A best-possible time for each gender and ages 8 to 100 is considered 100%. That time is the world record for each age, and if you're anywhere close to that blazing speed you can expect to win a gold medal at the next international competition! More realistically, 60% is considered locally competitive, 70% regional class, 80% national medal potential, and 90% internationally competitive. Below 60% will still make you healthy and more fit. You might be surprised to find your percentage is lower than you imagined. That can become a personal challenge to edge upward, fraction by fraction, using the number like a carrot on a string dangling in front of you. If your percentage is higher than you thought possible, you'll gain more self-confidence to train harder. You can also use a percentage calculated from the same

Table 2.2   1-Mile Walking Standards

Women

Age	%						
	100	90	80	70	60	50	40
20–29	6:10	6:51	7:42	8:48	10:16	12:20	15:25
30	6:10	6:51	7:42	8:48	10:16	12:20	15:25
35	6:21	7:03	7:56	9:04	10:35	12:42	15:52
40	6:35	7:18	8:13	9:24	10:58	13:10	16:27
45	6:51	7:36	8:33	9:47	11:25	13:42	17:07
50	7:08	7:55	8:55	10:11	11:53	14:16	17:50
55	7:28	8:17	9:20	10:40	12:26	14:56	18:40
60	7:50	8:42	9:47	11:11	13:03	15:40	19:35
65	8:16	9:11	10:20	11:48	13:46	16:32	20:40
70	8:46	9:44	10:57	12:31	14:36	17:32	21:55
75	9:21	10:23	11:41	13:21	15:35	18:42	23:22

Men

Age	%						
	100	90	80	70	60	50	40
20–29	5:33	6:10	6:56	7:55	9:15	11:06	13:52
30	5:33	6:10	6:56	7:55	9:15	11:06	13:52
35	5:43	6:21	7:08	8:10	9:31	11:26	14:17
40	5:55	6:34	7:23	8:27	9:51	11:50	14:47
45	6:07	6:47	7:38	8:44	10:11	12:14	15:17
50	6:22	7:04	7:57	9:05	10:36	12:44	15:55
55	6:38	7:22	8:17	9:28	11:03	13:16	16:35
60	6:57	7:43	8:41	9:55	11:35	13:54	17:22
65	7:18	8:06	9:07	10:25	12:10	14:36	18:15
70	7:42	8:33	9:37	11:00	12:50	15:24	19:15
75	8:10	9:04	10:12	11:40	13:36	16:20	20:25

distance to compare your times with someone older or younger; you might find that someone older who is slower might actually be "faster" since his or her percentage is higher than yours!

Here's how to calculate exact percentages for different 1-mile times than those presented in the table:

1. Convert your time into seconds by multiplying the minutes by 60, then adding the seconds to the total. For example, an 11:05 mile would be $11 \times 60 = 660$ seconds $+ 5$ seconds $= 665$ seconds.

2. Convert the 100% time on the table into seconds.

3. Divide the 100% time by your time. For a 50-year-old woman for example,

$$7:08 \div 11:05 =$$
$$428 \text{ seconds} \div 665 \text{ seconds} =$$
$$.64 \times 100 = 64\%$$

ASSESS YOUR WALKING TECHNIQUE

Obviously a full analysis of your technique without the help of trained eyes can be difficult. Still, I'd like you to do what you can to honestly assess your current technique. If anyone in your area is a capable walker, he or she can help assess your style.

You can videotape yourself walking on a track, standing in front of a mirror and "walking in place," watching yourself as you walk past buildings with large plate glass walls or windows, videotaping yourself on a treadmill, and watching yourself on a treadmill with nearby mirrors. Most advisable would be to do some combination of the above to get many views. A videotape can be handy to compare your technique as it improves.

The best way to see what you look like is to have someone videotape you walking (or set up a camera on a tripod or chair as you circle a track so it catches you each time around). A picture is truly worth a thousand words. The best angle, if you have someone holding a camera, is near a turn (figure 2.1) so the camera will catch you full-length coming toward it, pan with you—catching a full-body shot including the feet—as you move past, then film you from behind as you head off into the distance again. Make sure your cameraperson fills the frame with your image without cutting off any body parts. That way you'll see how you move as close-up as possible. And don't be shocked by what you see. You'll probably wonder—as most people do—who that strange person on the screen is who claims to be you.

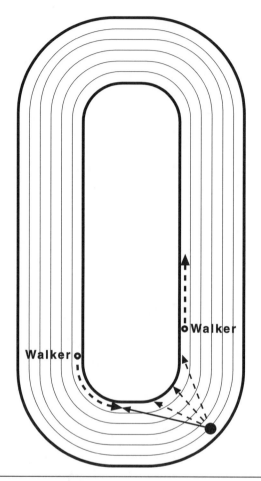

Figure 2.1 Videotaping from the correct vantage point will allow you to obtain a useful video for technique analysis. Shooting from the vantage point shown will allow you to videotape someone walking toward you, from the side, and walking away from you.

If you stand in front of a mirror, try to move as if you were walking, allowing your heels alternately to pop up off the ground in opposition to your arms.

Use this checklist to help you do a simplistic analysis of the technique you saw on yourself from the top down. You might even want to get someone else to offer an unbiased opinion.

☑ Is your head steady without rocking, bobbing, or swaying?

☑ Are your shoulders relaxed?

☑ Is your chin pulled in so your ears are over your shoulders?
☑ Are your arms bent, and do they remain at a 90-degree angle?
☑ Do your elbows stay tucked close to your waist?
☑ Are your fingers relaxed?
☑ Do your wrists stay strong, keeping your hands in a straight line with your arms?
☑ Is your back straight without a sway?
☑ Are your abdominals tight and pulled in?
☑ Are your hips loose and moving with your legs?
☑ Do your feet land strongly on your heels with toes lifted?
☑ Is your stride length controlled and smooth?
☑ From the side, do you look as if you're smoothly floating?

In addition to the above basic checklist, take an unbiased look at yourself. Even with an untrained eye, you can make some honest judgments about how you move, whether you look smooth or jerky, whether you look relaxed or tense, and whether you look quick-footed or loping. Write down any personal judgments.

Remember, too, that everyone has a certain amount of asymmetry to their body. You will always shoot for the ideal technique and try to balance your movement, but everyone must accept a modest amount of imbalance.

ASSESS YOUR GOALS

Not everyone wants to race, but every one of you wants to improve your performance or conditioning. Honestly assessing your short-term and long-term goals will help you recognize what kind of training plan you want to undertake.

Decide how important walking is to you to determine how much time you'll invest in training. Obviously, if you'd like to become a national-class athlete, you'll need several hours each day, not counting weightlifting sessions, massages, planning nutritional meals, and so on. Other training programs might only demand several hours a week. Be truthful with yourself about the number of hours you have available to you after mandatory weekly obligations that might include 40-hour workweeks, school, and family.

One woman approached me not long ago about wanting to walk a marathon in 10 weeks, but said she worked over 12 hours a day and could only train infrequently. I had to tell her I couldn't in good faith

put her on a program because with so little time to prepare she'd only be setting herself up for injury.

First, set short-term goals—striding your personal 3-mile workout course 90 seconds faster, walking a local weekend 2-mile race in a personal-best time, or completing a short-distance judged race walk without being disqualified.

Then set long-term goals—going from an age-graded percentage on your 1-mile walk of 55% to 65%, competing in a national master's track and field championship, or walking next year's local half marathon.

Those goals might change, too, so they'll need reassessing every few months. I never dreamed of being side by side on a racecourse with national champions, but suddenly there I was.

Knowing your goals will help you progress more realistically and more quickly.

ASSESS YOUR EXPERIENCE

If you don't already keep a log in which you can flip back a few pages to check your past experience, you'll need to take a few weeks to write down your walking and workout experience. Don't trust your memory. If you have even a slightly competitive spirit, the numbers you remember will skew upward. Assuming you have more walking experience, strength, and endurance than you do can lead to injuries, since your workouts and program will be based on your background.

1. How long have you been
   walking? _____ years/months/weeks

2. How far do you usually
   walk? _____ miles

3. How many days a week
   do you walk? _____ days per week

4. How fast do you usually _____ - minute miles/
   walk? miles per hour

5. What is your total weekly
   mileage? _____ miles per week

6. How often do you do
   strength work, such as
   lifting weights? _____ times per week

7. How often do you participate
   in other endurance/fitness
   sports activities such as
   cycling or aerobics? _____ times per week

8. How many total days per
   week do you exercise
   aerobically, other than
   walking? _____ days per week

This quick, informal analysis of your walking and fitness experience clearly lays out the workout foundation you possess and will help you design your own corresponding walking workouts and program based on safe and effective training principles.

Now that you've assessed your speed, technique, goals, and experience, it's time to work on the specifics of walking and race walking technique.

CHAPTER 3

WALKING
TECHNIQUE

Beginning walkers have only to put one foot in front of the other, with little thought to *how* they move. For improved performance and increased speed, however, fine-tuning your walking biomechanics is vital.

"I thought I knew how to walk!" my good friend and fellow journalist Teresa Watanabe wailed, walking beside me as I verbally poked and prodded her technique, which she had requested. I do. After only a few dozen meters, she felt the difference in her muscles and work output. She did know how to walk to transport herself around town, but not correctly or efficiently enough to get a real walking workout. Walking for performance is different than walking for perambulation, she discovered.

Using your muscles and joints correctly will allow you to apply all their power and strength to moving forward faster and over longer distances. That's because correct biomechanical movements for any skill-based sport or activity, such as fast walking, are also the most efficient ones in their use of oxygen and muscle fibers. Using efficient movements allows you to walk longer distances because you won't tire as quickly. Correct biomechanics will also usually mean fewer strained muscles or sprained ligaments.

Good walking technique, in other words, isn't just a way to complicate a simple activity. Instead, it allows you to maintain simplicity while reaching new levels of performance. For example, people who occasionally play miniature golf wouldn't say they are performance golfers. But even with minimal golf technique, they can hit the ball a few yards and have some fun. If they wanted to graduate to performance or competitive golf, they would take lessons and practice. You can say the same for walking: Beginning walking is like miniature golf, and fast walking is like playing 18 holes. You must learn about technique and then practice frequently, because fast walking well takes skill, body awareness, and kinesthetic sense—just like good golf does.

Like any other skilled activity, walking takes time to perfect. Like golfers, walkers are always learning more, honing style, smoothing out rough edges, watching others who are better, and trying to break bad habits. You wouldn't expect a hole-in-one your first day on the course; nor can you be impatient when you are learning walking technique. Not only are you learning new muscle patterns, but you might also be using new muscles, or even challenging familiar muscles in ways that are unfamiliar.

One San Jose area student of mine, Claire Raymond, had been a runner but had to give that up in her early 40s because of degenerative disc disease. She tried walking but couldn't go fast enough to break the sweat that, for her, meant she was getting a real heart-pumping workout. After one class, a few minor corrections, and a big verbal prod, she was roaring down the street in less than a 12-minute mile race walk. And she broke the sweat she loved. "My hair got wet," she said, "and that let me know I was getting my heart rate up."

The problem was, she was using different muscles in different ways than she was used to. So although she could find her high-performance aerobic walking pace, she couldn't maintain it—yet. So she practiced diligently, several times a week, and entered a couple of novice race walk events. Within a few months, her body accepted and thrived on the movement.

The message is, give yourself more than a day or a week to learn performance walking technique. Allow yourself at least 3 or 4 months of regular walking to build enough muscular strength and the motor patterns needed to feel comfortable with the technique and speed.

ENERGY CONSUMPTION

Fast walking can work wonders on your cardiovascular fitness, muscle tone, and calorie use, perhaps even more than running. Recall when you've tried to walk faster and how hard it seemed. Probably your leg muscles fatigued before you tired cardiovascularly. Most likely, an urge welled up deep inside that was heard as a little whisper in your head: "Run! It'll be easier." Maybe you did, and you discovered it was easier. If you didn't run, you probably quickly slowed your walking pace.

Here's the secret: For most people, the body naturally wants to break into a run somewhere around a 12- to 13-minute mile pace because it takes less muscle, and therefore less energy, to bounce along at an 11- or 12-minute mile jog than to walk powerfully at the same pace. You, as a walker who resisted the little voice, were forced to use extra muscle to keep yourself on the ground, to propel yourself forward with strong, muscular contractions in your legs and gluteals, and to move your legs faster to walk faster (more steps per minute, or higher "turnover," a term you'll hear several times).

The muscular contractions force your body to consume more oxygen, raise your heart rate, and demand more energy (i.e., calories) to sustain the activity. You probably also began to push toward and above your anaerobic threshold—the point where your body switches from primarily aerobic to primarily anaerobic energy—which increases your fitness and performance ability.

So let's take a closer look at how many calories fast walking uses compared to slower walking or running. First, the energy your body uses while walking increases linearly, keeping even pace with your speed progression until you reach that 12-minute barrier I discussed. Then the line shoots upward more sharply, although your pace still progresses linearly. For example, going from a 15-minute mile pace to a 12-minute mile pace increases your calorie use per minute about 50%. Stepping up to a 10-minute mile from a 15-minute mile approximately doubles your calorie use per minute.

In contrast to walking's exponential increases in energy demands with speed, running's energy use stays static, with your body consuming approximately the same number of calories per minute at whatever speed. Obviously as you go faster, you'll cover more ground and stay on your feet longer so caloric expenditure still jumps, but not like it does with walking. You can see an illustration of the differences between walking and running in figure 3.1. Note how walking's energy consumption surpasses running's at identical speeds once you pass the 12-minute mile barrier.

Note that I've said "per minute," meaning that if you walk 2 miles in 30 minutes at a 15-minute mile pace, you can't still settle for a 2-mile walk once you're faster, because you'll be on your feet less time, and

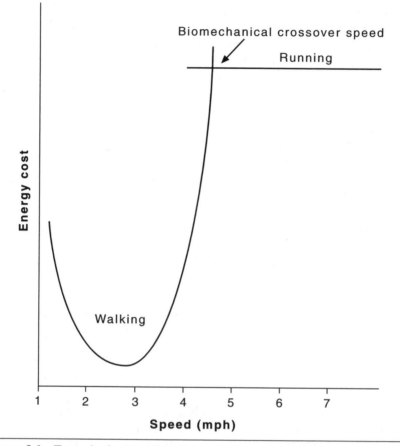

Figure 3.1 Typical relationship between speed and energy cost of walking and running. Note walking's steep rise in energy demand as speed increases versus running's linear requirement for energy.
Adapted from Hreljac 1993.

your calorie use won't be as high as you might like. Try instead to walk the same length of time (for example, now covering 2 1/2 miles in 30 minutes at a 12-minute mile pace) to accomplish your goals.

Let's now use a real-life comparison of one person who runs and walks. We'll use a 140-pound exerciser who is moderately fit and a relatively fast walker. In one workout, she walks a 12-minute mile pace for an hour and uses about 465 calories. The next day, she runs moderately at a 9-minute mile pace, but she can only keep that up for 30 minutes, using 360 calories. Note she's used 30% more calories on her walk.

If expending additional calories to lose body fat or body weight isn't important to you, then just know that the more energy you expend through increased muscular work, the stronger and more fit you will become. The stronger and more fit you become, the better the performances you will achieve and the quicker you'll attain any competitive goals you have. Even runners can cross train with fast walking as a way to log more miles without running's impact while still achieving a solid cardiovascular workout.

No matter who you are, or what your goals, knowledge of the biomechanics and technique of walking will get you there in less time.

THREE PHASES OF THE WALKING GAIT

Fast walkers using good technique will maximize the use of their levers (arms and legs) in the three biomechanical phases of walking as illustrated in figure 3.2. Good technique serves to conserve mechanical energy that is needed to keep speeds high without exhaustion setting in. No matter how fast you go, these phases are part of your stride, and learning more about them can help shed light on the finer points of performance walking's technique demands.

BRAKING

This is the phase where your heel strikes the ground in front of you, causing a millisecond of slowing of your stride as you gather your energy to bring your body's center of gravity up and over the foot. It is also one phase that incorporates "double support," meaning both feet contact the ground at the same time. Walkers try to minimize the braking by allowing their striking heel to land closer underneath their body so they lose less forward motion by minimizing the body's inefficient up-and-down movement. Runners, who land on a bent knee, store energy in the muscles in this phase. That stored energy—or elastic energy—is then expended for propulsion to get them through the air in a subsequent flight phase, nonexistent in walking.

MIDSTANCE

This is where you are balancing for a moment on one leg—also called a "single support" or "swing" phase—while your body is nearly vertical. The nonsupporting leg is relaxed and being carried through from rear to front with the knee bent. This is a moment of pure relaxation of upper and lower body where race walkers allow their nonweight-bearing hip to drop.

Figure 3.2 The three phases of the walking gait: (a) braking, (b) midstance, and (c) propulsive.

PROPULSIVE

This third phase could be considered the most vital for walkers. Walkers must rely heavily on propulsion from the rear foot to carry themselves faster, since they haven't stored elastic energy from running's bent-knee landing and following flight phase. In the propulsive phase, the rear leg is extended for a moment while the ball of the foot remains on the ground and the heel is lifted high. The front heel has already contacted the ground, making this another moment of double support.

As I delve into the intricacies of correct walking biomechanics within these phases, remember that everybody will develop a personal style along the spectrum of good technique. Some will look graceful, some less so. Some will always have one shoulder that pops up and down, or a head that bobs to the right. Avoid beating yourself up to be the perfect walker, because there is no such thing as perfect. Teach your body the best way to move to reach your goals. Never be afraid to listen to a critique from someone new that might help fix a bad habit. But if you're accomplishing what you want without getting hurt, go with it. Walking is not like dancing in the corps de ballet where everyone's eyelashes and toenails must move identically. Walking is a dance of individualism within the three distinct biomechanical phases.

TECHNIQUE: STEP BY STEP

Really good walkers move like great models—smoothly and elegantly. You won't notice any one body part, just a purring machine sliding down the trail in a seemingly effortless symphony of movement. Long-time race walkers have said that if you see a good walker from the opposite side of a tall hedge, you'd think the person is on a skateboard because his or her head stays on one plane.

Kids are great at learning good walking technique. They just watch and imitate. As adults, we think so hard—too hard really. Although I will get very analytical in our breakdown that follows, read it all through, then just go try it without engaging too many brain cells. Walking novices who overintellectualize end up walking like Frankenstein—stiffly, like they've just risen from the dead, with the right arm going with the right leg and the left arm with the left leg.

So pour this discussion into your brain—maybe stand up and try a few things as you read—then go do it. Come back and read it again. You'll see something new every time you pick up this section again. As you go through the material on technique, it will be a good time to review the videotape you took of yourself walking, as suggested in chapter 2. Watch for each item as I discuss it. One more tip: If there are knowledgeable, skilled walkers in your area, find them, watch them, and walk with them. Watching live action can help you better fine-tune the technique you will read about.

RELAXATION

Good walking is the pinnacle of total relaxation. If you're not relaxed, you'll be working harder than you need to and expending more energy while going more slowly than you want. Relaxed walking should feel loose and comfortable. Shoulders, arms, hands, legs, hips, knees, toes—everything should be relaxed. You want to walk well, but don't try too hard at it. Otherwise you, too, could look like a Frankenstein-style novice.

Try the following for added relaxation in your technique before, during, or after your walk:

- Roll both shoulders backward, alternating sides. Lift the shoulder upward, pull it backward to open your chest, pull it downward, then let it roll forward. Repeat several times on each side.

- Pull your shoulders up toward your ears, tensing and holding for a few seconds. Then release completely, and let them drop loosely and unassisted.

- Stand on one leg and shake the other gently so you feel the loose muscles jiggle up and down your leg. Especially feel the looseness in the joint where your thigh bone connects to your pelvic girdle.

- Shake out your arms as you did your legs. Try this several times during a walk to release tension that develops in your arms and shoulders from the strong arm carriage.

- Practice backstroke arms (figure 3.3) to release your shoulders. Either one at a time, or alternating together, swing each extended arm loosely through the full range of motion. The hand starts down at your side, pulls straight ahead of you, rotates through a skyward-pointing position with the arm next to your head, pulls straight back with the elbow nearly extended, then returns to the start at your side. Also try this with a slow walk with your right arm going up as your left foot steps forward and your left arm going up as your right foot steps forward.

Figure 3.3 The backstroke arm-swing exercise loosens the shoulder as you move your arm: (a) straight ahead of the chest, (b) next to the ear pointing skyward, and (c) behind the body as the arm completes a full circle.

POSTURE

Think proud. Slouching or chin-jutting could lead to tight, strained, or achy upper-body muscles. Your head should be pulled tall, as if someone had a grip on the hair on the crown of your head and was pulling upward. Keep your chin lifted and pulled inward so your ears are over your shoulders. Your eyes may cast downward about 3 to 4 yards ahead of your toes, but only if your head stays upright. Shoulders are held back with chest open and lifted. Abdominals are pulled tight to support your back and add power to your leg propulsion.

In some cases, postural imbalances that inhibit your success at standing tall are caused by years of holding muscles a particular way. They often can't be corrected overnight, since they and their opposing muscle groups will need to be stretched and strengthened to bring the skeleton back into correct alignment. Consult with a fitness trainer, sports doctor, or physical therapist for exercises to suit your needs.

Meanwhile, try this as one way (figure 3.4) to help you find any muscular imbalances that might cause slouching:

Stand with your back to a wall. The back of your head, the back of your shoulders, and your buttocks and heels are also against the wall. You should be able to fit your hand between your low back and the wall, but it should be a snug fit. If there's too much room, tighten your abdominals and tuck your hips slightly, without bending your knees, as if trying to flatten your low back against the wall. The hip tuck is called a posterior tilt of the pelvis.

Remain in this tall position for a few moments and sense any discomfort. Tightness or discomfort in one part of your body, such as your shoulders, neck, or back, might indicate muscular imbalances that need attention.

If you are a woman you need to be aware of keeping your shoulders and chest open. Many of us have the tendency to roll our shoulders forward in a slightly chest-protective posture. This can crimp our oxygen transport and cause muscle tension and strain.

ARM AND HAND POSITION

Fast walking needs powerful propulsion from the arms and back muscles. So although your appendages are relaxed, you will actively engage the muscles in your back that move them, since they are counterbalances to the legs. Many fitness walkers can accomplish a

Figure 3.4 Check your posture using the wall as a guide.

great deal by simply bending their arms at the elbow in a 90-degree angle (no larger) and using them actively rather than carrying them passively.

Maintain that right angle as if your arm were in a cast. Allow your elbow to push straight backward until the hand, held in a loose fist, reaches your hip bone directly to your side (figure 3.5a). On the forward swing, the hand should reach no higher than your nipple line (figure 3.5b) and should not cross the midline of your body, although it may swing inward slightly toward the center (figure 3.5c). The movement should come from the shoulder, never from the elbow.

Figure 3.5 Correct arm and hand position throughout the swing requires that the elbow maintain a 90-degree angle while: (a) to the rear the hand stops at the hip bone, and (b) to the front it stops at the nipple line. The hand should not cross the midline of the body (c).

Although the hand position will vary from walker to walker, your hands at their highest forward point will be approximately 8 to 10 inches in front of your chest.

Your elbows should feel as if they are pinched slightly inward to avoid resembling a chicken with wings flapping widely side to side. As you swing your arm forward and backward, give the elbow a strong push to the rear as if you were trying to elbow someone directly behind you. As the arm moves forward, you should feel a strong punch to the front of you with the hand, without reaching forward or extending your elbow.

Using your arms decisively to the front and back will actually help your feet and legs move with more power and speed. Basic physics will tell you that, for example, as you accelerate your right arm to the front, you will create a force in the opposite direction, in this case one that begins at your hip and continues down your leg to your right foot as it pushes to the rear. And as you decelerate your right arm so you can begin to move it to the rear, the force you create goes in the reverse direction, that is, to the front; this helps keep your body moving forward. A powerful arm swing means powerful walking.

Then come hands, which may be held in many ways. The most common, however, is a loose fist with the palm toward your body's midline. Imagine you're holding a raw egg or a newborn kitten so you don't start to tense and grip. The more muscle power you put into tension, the less you'll have for your workout. You should also avoid cocking from the wrist inward or outward; rather, you should try to keep your hand aligned with your forearm. If you notice strange aches in your forearm or wrist after a workout, perhaps you are unwittingly holding your hand tensely outward or inward.

Try this at home:

Stand in front of a mirror and bend your arms to a 90-degree angle at the elbow. Now begin to swing them forward and backward. Watch the motion closely, analyzing for elbows flapping outward, hand position too high or crossing the midline to the front, arms carried at too wide an angle so your hands drop too low, weak or cocked wrist position, and bobbing shoulders. Try to correct the action as you watch yourself.

Also, try speeding up the swing to see if you can keep a smooth, efficient movement at a faster pace. You can also turn with your side to the mirror to make sure your hand does not go beyond your buttocks on the action to the rear. Be sure to watch both sides, since many people will move differently on each side.

Practice this regularly to put a stop to bad habits before it's too late.

Try this while on a walk:

Walk close to a tall fence or hedge so your elbow when tucked in properly is not quite touching it. If your elbows knock or brush against it as you move, you're probably allowing them to swing too far outward, rather than tucking them in to your sides and swinging them backward.

STRIDE LENGTH

One of the keys to getting faster is finding the stride length that's right for you. Most walkers tend to overstride, an inefficient motion causing them to bounce up and down with each step. Overstriders reach in front of them with each step, creating a longer braking phase and more wasted energy that could be better used in forward motion. The increased impact of each step also produces more potentially harmful skeletal jarring. Remember the race walker's analogy of the walker looking as if he or she were on wheels? You should roll along without feeling as if you're clomping or stomping.

Find the smooth roll of a good stride length (figure 3.6). Then try quick steps because walkers, to go faster, increase the speed of their "turnover," or the number of steps per minute, rather than increasing stride length, or the amount of ground they cover per step with long steps to the front. Studies have shown that runners, as they speed up, insignificantly increase their steps per minute, but increase their stride length considerably. Walkers, on the other hand, can go from 120 steps per minute for fitness walkers to race walking highs of 220 or more steps per minute. One study showed runners at 8 kilometers per hour (7:25-mile pace) doing 166 steps per minute, while race walkers at 8.1 kilometers per hour (7:24-mile pace) produced a stride rate of 185 (Cairns, 1986)!

Some novice walkers assume that you need long legs to go faster. How wrong they are! Long legs are, in fact, a disadvantage. If the goal is to create higher leg turnover, then the longer the limb (i.e. lever), the longer it will take to move through its arc, which could slow turnover. Longer legs, therefore, require a walker to work harder to not lope through the stride and waste energy. Many successful national-class race walkers actually have long torsos and what appear to be disproportionately short legs, a build that allows them to move more efficiently with speed.

Figure 3.6 Good stride length.

Whatever their length, it's important to move your legs as smoothly and as quickly as possible. Try this to feel the difference in stride lengths and help you find yours:

First, take extra-long, overexaggerated strides for about 40 yards, allowing yourself to bounce. Think galloping, loping, sloppy, and slow (figures 3.7a and b). Then take teeny, mincing steps for 40 yards (figures 3.7c and d). These should feel awkward, be nearly heel to toe, and lacking in any power. Then alternate the pattern, taking overly long steps for about 10 yards and mincing steps for about 10 yards, repeating twice.

Now take overly long steps, then tiny steps, then float into a smooth gait between over-long and tiny steps without bouncing

Figure 3.7 Help find your correct stride length by feeling what's wrong first: (a) and (b) walk with long, overexaggerated strides, and (c) and (d) short, mincing steps.

or mincing. Repeat several times so your body knows the difference. It can be difficult to perceive how your own body is moving, so try this with a buddy so you can watch each other.

Interestingly, if your arm swing is too big, then your stride will also follow suit, since upper and lower limbs will synchronize (figure 3.8). If you can't seem to smooth out and bring your stride length under control, take another look at your arm swing.

HEEL STRIKE AND FOOT PLACEMENT

Walkers land squarely on the heel of the lead leg. In comparison, slower runners land on the midsole, while faster runners and sprinters land on their toes. The lifting of the toes at heel strike (figure 3.9) will allow you to use the full range of motion in the ankle joint to produce

Figure 3.8 Bad stride length with overreaching arms and legs.

Figure 3.9 Good heel strike and toe lift.

more power as you roll through the flat-footed midstance phase and into the propulsive pushoff phase with heel lifted.

Technically speaking, in a fast walk the foot will land slightly on the heel's lateral edge. It will then roll along its outside edge toward the toes, before rolling back to its midline at the ball and pushing off with the middle toes. Most people will do this naturally with their feet, just like breathing. If you think too hard about the foot's roll-through, you'll probably end up walking like Frankenstein once again. Know what's most accurate, but just walk. Worry about corrections only if they are needed.

Once you begin to master the heel strike with toe lifted, the tibialis anterior and peroneal muscles in the front and side of your lower leg (shin) might begin to burn or ache. This is not a bad thing. In fact, it will show you're doing the technique correctly. The ache is not likely what is commonly called "shin splints." Your muscles are simply being asked to lift the toes repeatedly (remember those 120+ steps per minute?), something they're not used to doing.

In chapter 6, I will address some strengthening and stretching exercises for your training program. For now, get out the ice bag after your workout until the muscles get strong enough to handle your developing technique. If, however, the ache continues several hours after you're done walking, you might consider seeing a sports doctor.

In addition, walk with your toes pointed straight ahead, not pointed outward or toed in, because that will allow the most efficient use of your foot action to move forward. Any outward or inward placement of the foot will not allow you to cover ground as quickly (figure 3.10). Imagine this: If your toes are pointed straight ahead, you might cover 10 inches per foot strike. If they're pointed slightly outward, you might cover 9 1/2 inches per foot strike. If you're walking 150 steps per minute, you will cover 6 feet, 3 inches less per minute, which would translate into a loss of 75 feet, or about 11 seconds, over one 12-minute mile!

Try this to practice a good heel strike and toe lift:
Walk 30 or 40 yards using shorter and quicker steps than usual, but allowing your feet to land with toes lifted high. Rest your shins by walking a short distance on your toes with heels high. Repeat several times.

Try this exercise to practice walking with your toes straight:
Walk with a track lane line or a line in a road between your feet. Cast your eyes, not your chin, downward to see if your feet parallel the line, or turn inward or outward.

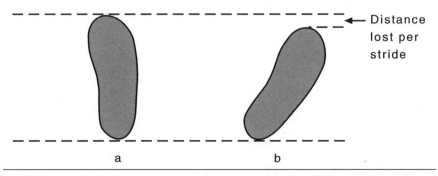

Figure 3.10 Proper foot placement with toe aligned (a) and improper foot placement with the toe out (b). Even slightly toeing out or in can force you to lose precious inches or power.

PUSHOFF

Walkers aren't able to rely on elastic energy stored in their muscles from a bent-knee landing, nor do they use the stored energy to propel them into the air and forward like runners. Therefore, discovering a solid pushoff with your rear leg and foot means everything for stronger walking performance.

To help find a stronger pushoff, you should feel as if your leg is extending fully to the rear with each step. The heel should stay on the ground as long as possible. When it does come up, you should roll through the entire foot, dynamically pushing the ball of the foot and the toes against the ground as they roll off (figure 3.11). You will probably feel your buttocks contract to aid the push.

Avoid "snowshoe walking." In snowshoe walking the rear foot lifts passively with one gigantic motion as if you can't bend the foot because it's attached to a snowshoe and you need huge clearance to carry it through to the front.

Figure 3.11 Good pushoff.

Unlike snowshoe walking, a good pushoff creates a perfect example of Newton's Third Law of Physics: Every action is opposed by an equal and opposite reaction. In this case, the force of your pushing backward against the ground causes a reaction of propelling your body forward, and the greater the force of your push, the greater the propulsion.

Feeling the pushoff can indeed be a challenge, but knowing how your body and muscles should feel will help. Watching a videotape of yourself helps tremendously, too, especially if more experienced walkers happen to pass through so you can compare your technique to theirs.

Try this exercise to feel the pushoff:

Position yourself in a standing lunge position with one leg in front of the other, the front knee bent and the rear knee straight. Place your hands on a wall (or other, similar object) in front of you. Now lift the heel of the rear foot, keeping the rear leg straight and pretend you're trying to push the wall away from you (figure 3.12).

Figure 3.12 The standing lunge and pushoff exercise can help you feel a correct walking pushoff.

Notice the force that's created between the ball of the rear foot and the ground. That is the pushoff for performance walking.

These exercises will also help you feel the pushoff:

Choose a hill or slight incline that's at least 30 yards long. With the best walking technique you have so far, walk quickly up the hill. Notice how with each step you are forced to push yourself forward with the rear foot to move uphill. That is the feeling you'll translate into level walking.

The next exercise is worth experimenting with because it helps you feel a contrast enabling you to know when you aren't pushing off correctly. Although this exercise can also train good body position, the lean you'll feel can help you feel a pushoff. You can do this as a part of your warm-up or cooldown, or during your walk to remind yourself of correct pushoff. Be sure to keep your abdominals tight to support your back.

Walking along a flat surface, try three body positions as you're moving, with the difference in angle coming from your feet and ankles, not from your waist, back, or shoulders:

1. Lean backward as you walk. Sense that it's a bit of a struggle to move forward; also feel the lack of momentum and the decrease in power from your rear foot (figure 3.13a).

2. Walk as straight up and down as possible. Again, sense the lack of forward momentum (figure 3.13b).

3. Walk with a slight forward lean from your ankles, being certain to keep your body aligned and butt tucked in. Allow your rear foot to push yourself into a forward fall with each step (figure 3.13c).

Repeat all three body positions for a few yards each, smoothly transitioning from one to the other so your body feels the difference. Talk yourself through it if it helps.

HIP MOVEMENT

Most of our discussion of hip movement will be reserved for the specifics of race walking technique, but if you are looking for increased speed and performance you should also allow your hips to move naturally from the low back and through the pelvic girdle. This doesn't necessarily mean adopting the highly visible pelvic roll of race walking. It just means letting your legs and hips move freely without locking your body stiffly in place between the waist and thighs.

Figure 3.13 Allow your body to experience both an incorrect and correct body lean and push: (a) lean backward from the feet as you walk, (b) walk straight up, and (c) walk with a slight forward lean from the ankles.

This movement is not so unusual. Watch people moving along the street or strolling park trails. What you'll see in most is a natural forward and backward movement of the hips; when the right leg steps forward the right hip bone follows slightly, requiring the opposite leg to stay to the rear. With that hip staying to the rear, its rotation must be slightly open.

All you need to do is simply relax through the lower part of the body and let your hips move. More technical hip instruction goes with race walking technique which follows.

Now that we've been through all the pieces to help you walk faster—and you've probably tried them out a few times—you may have developed a little muscle soreness. That's typical of anyone trying a new activity or giving it more energy than before, as long as you're sore in the right places.

There are correct places to be sore—for example, calves if you're pushing off, feet if you're rolling through, shins if you're heel-striking with toes lifted, hamstrings and gluteals if you're pushing off with the entire leg, and latissimus dorsi in your middle back if you're swinging your arms strongly. You might feel your adductors in your inner thigh, since they too help flex the hip joint in carrying the leg to the front, and you might find your biceps are sore from carrying your arms longer than normal in a bent position.

There are also incorrect places to be sore and some possible technique flaws producing the ache: tops of shoulders (from tensing them upward), heels (insufficient shoe cushioning or too hard of a heel strike), forearms (from gripping your hands in a fist), back of neck (from jutting your chin forward), and low back (from a swayback). Any ache or soreness that doesn't go away in about 3 days might need extra attention from a sports doctor.

RACE WALKING: AN EXTRA STEP

When you first try race walking technique, you might identify with Susan Heiser, a race walker now living in the Portland, Oregon area. When she began race walking, she usually scheduled her workouts after sunset. Why? As much as she liked the sport, she thought she looked silly, so she was a closet walker, so to speak, hiding behind the cloak of darkness. I've known a few others like that. I've also known walkers who break into runs around other people—especially teenage boys—because they don't want to be ridiculed. I've always kept right on striding—in the light of day and past groups of kids. The best treatment with kids is to challenge them to walk with you. Usually they can't keep up.

Those who have tried it usually appreciate how much more energy it takes to walk fast than to jog moderately. One time a few years ago I was race walking a 10-kilometer road run. A runner fell into step beside me (I was doing just under a 9-minute mile pace), uttered some admiring words, then said, "I tried that once. But it was too hard." I take that as a compliment because I'm doing something the runner gave up on.

Although race walking can attract gawks of wonderment and a few giggles, the technique is mostly everyday walking taken to an extreme, a style needed to allow smoother leg swings, faster steps, and less bouncing—all in the name of going even faster.

HIP ROTATION

Ask anyone what comes to mind when they think of race walking. Nine times out of 10, they'll swing their derriere side to side as a physical response to the question.

Therein lies the misconception. In race walking you do not actually—or are not supposed to—swing your hips from side to side reminiscent of Marilyn Monroe's sashay. As shown in figure 3.14, in the propulsive phase the hip (or pelvis) actually extends to the rear, rotating from the low back slightly on the longitudinal axis. Then it drops vertically as that leg is carried through the midstance phase to the front. Finally, the hip rotates slightly toward the body's midline as that heel swings to the front and is placed on the ground in the braking stance. "Oh, that must hurt your hips," onlookers sometimes tell race walkers. How mistaken they are. It's a flowing, natural motion that feels smooth and effortless.

Your hips, then, perform two distinct actions which you must consciously initiate: extension and what is called "drop." Hip flexion—the swing to the front—usually comes naturally.

The extending and dropping of the hips with each step help maintain the center of gravity on one plane, allowing you to move forward with less energy—because any vertical motion is eliminated—than such a high speed would normally require. In addition, the rotation of your hips allows you to cover more ground with each stride (figure 3.15) without the overstriding reach to the front and subsequent bounce. Again, the result is getting to the finish line—or just getting more fit—faster.

Figure 3.14 Correct hip rotation moves your hips through three phases: (a) an inwardly rotated and flexed position in the braking position at heel strike, (b) a relaxed position in midstance (while the opposite hip is dropped), and (c) an open and extended position during propulsion.

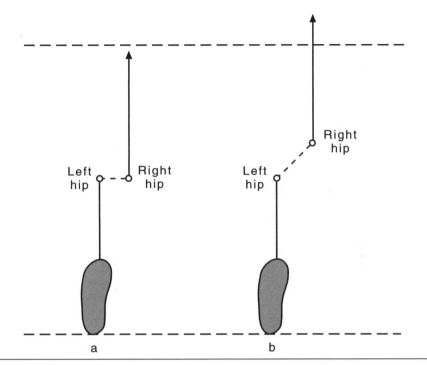

Figure 3.15   Note how someone who hasn't mastered a race walker's hip rotation (a) won't cover ground as quickly as someone who has (b).

Practice your hip motion in front of a mirror at home, progressing through this three-step exercise. Try not to think too hard once you understand the directions:

1. Stand with feet a little narrower than hip-width apart. Bend your arms in a 90-degree angle. Drive your right elbow backward, allowing your right hip bone to rotate to the front slightly in opposition to your rear-driving elbow. The left elbow will swing naturally forward in opposition. Swing gently forward and backward with the arms, allowing the hips to continue their opposing rotation.

2. Add your legs. When your right elbow drives backward and your right hip bone rotates forward, allow your right heel to pop off the ground. Your right knee will bend and turn inward slightly, while the left knee will remain extended. Try this a few times to each side, increasing to a natural speed.

3. Add a hip drop. When your right hip bone rotates forward with your right heel coming off the ground, allow that hip to drop slightly downward. The left hip will pull backward more

forcefully and feel as if it's lifting. The lift only comes from the extended left knee.

Do this progression several times, adding each piece gradually.

When you're out on walks, imagine that your leg doesn't begin where the thigh bone meets the pelvis (where it bends), but rather that it actually begins at your waist; allow your hip bone on each side to carry forward with each step as if it were part of the leg. In addition, pushing off strongly through the entire foot, as discussed previously, will naturally increase your hip extension.

SHOULDER MOVEMENT

The relaxed roll of your shoulders also stems from your hips' movement (also sometimes called *hip roll*) because when one part of your body moves, another must move in opposition. Allow shoulder movement to come naturally in response to your hips. The roll should feel like the backstroking arm exercise described earlier, only without your arms swinging.

To prepare your shoulders before a walk, try this:

Lift the right shoulder up and roll it backward while the left shoulder begins to move in opposition, starting to drop and roll forward. Continue this alternating roll for a minute or so.

FOOT PLACEMENT

Now that you have the hips extending, dropping, and rotating, I can discuss placing the feet heel to toe on a line, because it is only the rotation of the hips along the longitudinal axis that throws the foot naturally toward the midline of the body and creates the "balance-beam" foot placement. Not everyone will—or should—"walk a line" in foot placement. This is especially true of many women because of their wider pelvic girdle. Most walkers will at least come close to it without much thought as they place the inside of the right foot on the right side of an imaginary lane line, and the inside of the left foot along the left side of the lane line (figure 3.16). If you don't have some hip rotation, heel-to-toe foot placement shouldn't be forced.

There are a couple of reasons for streamlining the foot placement. The first is to keep the hips from rocking to the right and to the left over the feet, displacing the center of gravity side to side with each step. The second is to allow you to cover more ground with each step without overstriding which, as we've discussed, will displace the center of gravity up and down. Both displacements make for less efficient walking and will slow you down.

Direction of travel

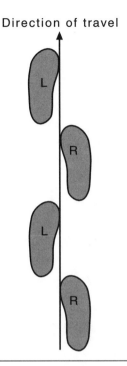

Figure 3.16 Let your foot placement come naturally as your hip roll progresses. Letting the insides of your feet touch an imaginary line can be more effective for some people than the classic heel-to-toe action.

A simple exercise will help you analyze your foot placement:

Walk along a line on the track, trail, or road. Keep your chin lifted, but glance down at your feet as you stride to check on their relationship to the line.

KNEE STRAIGHTENING

When discussing race walkers' hips, I mentioned the need to keep your knee extended to create a straight leg. If you want to race walk legally—perhaps participating in some judged races—then your knee must be straight when the heel first strikes the ground in front of you and must remain straight at least through the vertical, or stance, phase of your gait. You should avoid landing on a bent knee and leaving it bent as it passes under you, as depicted in figure 3.17. Obviously, if you have no interest in racing and being judged, you don't have to worry about exact straightening at the right times and may be perfectly happy with a slight bend at the knee joint. That isn't formal race walking, but simply speed walking, in which you can choose

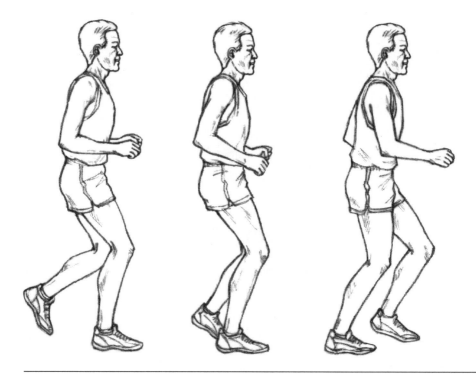

Figure 3.17 A walker with bent knees will appear to be jogging.
Adapted from USATF.

what's most comfortable. Beware, though, that walking in a continually over-crouched position can put an additional strain on your knees.

Despite the lack of a knee-straightening mandate unless you're racing, most people without orthopedic problems find the knee does indeed straighten in the vertical position for a split second even when strolling the mall or taking out the garbage. No matter what a person's goal or preference, it's frequently a natural part of the walking gait; if you don't straighten your knee, you are crouching (à la Groucho Marx) or you are running (if you add jumping into the air).

I advocate that you dedicate yourself to walking properly if you're going to walk fast, rather than do some mushy version of not-really-running because you aren't coming off the ground and not-really-walking because you're crouching along. You've perhaps seen someone who is moving along with feet so low to the ground that you can't determine if he or she is trying to race walk and can't, or is trying to run and is just slow. A low-foot bent-knee shuffle walk-run doesn't mandate the muscular contractions that make fast walking the workout that it is. Those who try this walk-run version often come away

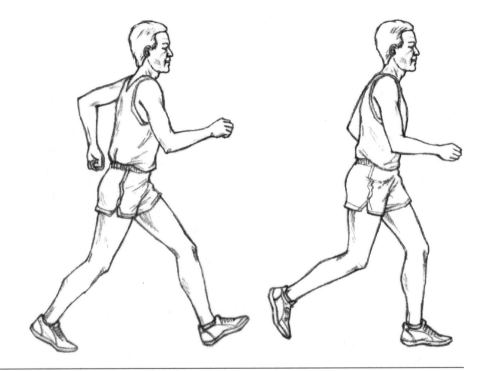

wondering why they didn't get a workout. Make the difference distinct because you will use more muscle and more oxygen, get a better workout, decrease your chance of injury, and increase your chance of getting faster.

Finally, remember that to race walk straighten your knees; you do not lock them or hyperextend them forcefully, both of which can damage your joints and the surrounding soft tissue. You should never feel your knee joint slamming backward.

If you are having trouble overcoming a bent-knee walk, you might need to focus on stretching your hamstrings in the back of your upper thighs and your calves in the lower leg, as well as strengthening the quadriceps and shins in the front of the leg.

Otherwise, to practice knee straightening:

Without worrying about your arms, lift the right foot slightly and place the heel (with the toes lifted high) directly in front of the left toe, straightening the leg with the downward placement. Alternate sides, dynamically placing each heel with toes lifted in front of the other. Make sure the steps are mincing.

Other postural concerns that can affect knee straightening will be addressed later in this chapter under the section on common mistakes.

LEG CARRIAGE

In another ill-fated attempt to move faster sooner than their biomechanics will allow, race walking novices often resort to lifting their knees too high. From a distance you'll look as if you're stepping over something in the road, or friends won't be sure if you're running or walking. Former runners sometimes develop this habit because good running technique requires a high knee lift. In contrast, walking mandates low knee carriage for utmost efficiency in carrying the long lever through its radius of motion. Pick up your feet only enough to clear the ground, with the foot transitioning from back to front next to the ankle. Imagine you are kicking a pebble along the ground in front of you to keep your knees and feet low and fast.

BUT ARE YOU RUNNING?

That's the strange feeling that many novice speed walkers express when they push themselves to the next level of performance: How can anyone go this fast without running? You can, and you will. To help soothe your concerns, either videotape yourself from the side or have a friend watch you. Make sure you're not leaping into the air between strides, landing on a bent knee, or bending your knee when it's directly beneath your body. You should always see a moment of double-limb support.

Watching and imitating are keys to successful fast walking. Find a way to watch real race walkers. Even if you never want to race, you'll expand your knowledge of technique and efficiency. Live action is worth a thousand words and pictures. Since race walking is shown so rarely on televised sports programs, you'll have to dig out races, events, and clubs in your area. We'll discuss how to plug yourself into the race walker's network in chapter 8, with a limited list of resources in appendix B.

ONE FINAL RACE WALKING EXERCISE

Now that we've drilled into you the minutiae of technique and analysis, take a moment to forget it all and try one simple exercise called a jog-to-walk:

Run easily and very slowly along a flat surface for 10 to 20 yards. Then, with one step, extend your knee in front of you, landing on a straightened leg as you transition into a quick-paced race walk. Keep the momentum you had in your run as you continue for another 10 to 20 yards. Think tall and let your body fall forward. Jog out of it, shake out your legs and arms. Repeat. If done properly, this can in one fell swoop allow your body to feel and incorporate into its muscle memory the sensation of fast walking.

COMMON TECHNIQUE ERRORS

Everyone will soon discover their walking idiosyncracies of posture and gait. No matter how good you become, you will have technique downfalls that you will revert to occasionally, especially when you're tired or slightly out of shape. That's why it's important to always stay tuned in to your body, videotape yourself again and again, and allow friends and walking companions to offer helpful critique if they notice a technique error.

Often, in their enthusiasm to go faster, novice fast walkers tend to revert to a handful of mistakes in technique. Know what they are, notice whether you fall prey, and learn to avoid them by continual technique monitoring, stretching, or strengthening. Some errors might be caused by congenital postural imbalances and lopsided muscular development, none of which are easily corrected, and could need the attention of a specialty physician, chiropractor, podiatrist, or physical therapist. In the following sections I'll discuss just a few of the more common flaws.

FORWARD LEAN

As a novice eager to get there faster, you might try to lead with your chest, leaning forward from your waist with your hips flexed (figure 3.18). Not only does that posture put a strain on your back and tighten your hip flexors, but it also slows you down. The power of the legs is limited by chopping off the heel strike, which forces a flat-footed landing, limits the range of motion of the foot's roll-through, and decreases the power of the pushoff. It's like a domino effect as all the pieces of your technique fall apart.

If you're interested in legal race walking, the additional problem of the forward lean is that it often forces the front knee to bend upon landing to support the torso's weight over it and soften the increased

Figure 3.18 Incorrect forward lean from the waist.

impact on the knee. That could lead to disqualification from a race, which isn't much fun.

Pull yourself into the tall posture discussed at the beginning of this chapter. Feel someone's hand pulling up on the imaginary rope that continues from your spine, up the back of your head, and out your crown.

Two postural weaknesses might, however, need to be addressed before you can correct this error safely.

1. **Weak abdominals.** The weakness could mean you aren't able to support an upright torso for an entire walk. You'll need to consult with a gym, personal trainer, or a good book (such as Dean and Greg Brittenham's *Stronger Abs and Back*) on strengthening exercises. In any case, correctly executed abdominal curls will strengthen your torso.

2. **Tight hip flexors.** In today's society, tight hip flexors are more
   common a curse than not because we spend so much time
   sitting down and shortening those muscles. Again, you'll need
   to perform a good stretch that isolates the hip flexors.

Once you're aware of the problem—and an ache in your back after
walks might be one clue of some technique error—work on walking tall
and use the preceding exercises.

SWAYBACK

This flaw, shown in figure 3.19, is often combined with the forward
lean, but can also be seen in those with an upright posture. It can put

Figure 3.19 Swayback posture.

pressure on your low back, which could cause pain, and can limit the hip rotation needed for race walking. Interestingly, a number of high-level race walkers actually walk with a moderate swayback. If you're pain free and have no limitation, it might not be a problem, but be aware it could develop into one.

Deficiencies in strength and flexibility in your abdominals (addressed before), hip flexors, low back, and hamstrings can contribute to a swayback walk.

Powerless Arms

Without a dynamic arm swing, you won't go very fast. Other than sprinters, most runners simply hang their arms slightly bent at their sides. They can get away with that because they have stored elastic energy from the knee bend to help them move forward. You can't just let the arms hang there because they need the power each swing generates to help forward propulsion.

You should feel the muscles in your back power the arms forward and backward. You should feel the elbow punch backward and the hand punch forward.

Try this to feel a powerful arm swing:

Have a friend or fellow walker stand behind or beside you. First, have your friend hold the palm of a hand in front of your chest as you try to box it (figure 3.20a). Then, have your friend hold the palm of a hand behind you so you can elbow it strongly (figure 3.20b).

You might also need to strengthen your back muscles, especially the latissimus dorsi, as well as your pectorals in the chest. Both help power the swing.

In addition, make sure you maintain the 90-degree bend of the elbow for full power. You'll find your forearms might begin to hang lower and lower during your walk as your biceps and shoulders tire if you aren't used to carrying your arms bent. Remind yourself now and then to keep them bent so you can keep the swing tight and fast, which will help keep your feet and legs moving as fast as you need.

Flying Elbows

There are two types of flying elbows. Some people call the first case of flying elbows "chicken wings." If you allow your elbows to fly outward as if you're jabbing people standing beside you, the energy will go from right to left rather than forward, dissipating your propulsion and

Figure 3.20 Have a friend help you develop a strong arm swing as you: (a) punch his or her palms to the front and (b) elbow his or her palms to the rear.

speed. If this is a trap you fall into, imagine you are pinching your waist with your elbows and trying to hold a binder between your arm and your upper torso. Likely, your arms will feel too tight to your torso, but since you're used to winging them outward, it'll probably be just right.

In the second case of flying elbows, your elbows stay close to your torso, but you flex and extend them with every swing, adding a bounce with your forearm and expending energy better spent in forward propulsion. Imagine your arm is in a cast and can't move except at the shoulder.

Try this to determine if you're flexing and extending your elbows:

Hang a long string or shoelace around your neck with the ends dangling down your chest. Bend your elbows in a 90-degree angle, and hold onto the string at the level of your hands. Now swing your arms. You shouldn't feel the string rubbing back and forth across the back of your neck. If you do, the elbows are alternately bending and unbending while pulling upward and downward.

Flap Feet and Flat Feet

Weak ankles, feet, and lower leg muscles can contribute to poor foot and leg work. You might "hear" yourself walking because your feet flap downward immediately after heel strike ("flap feet"), or you land flat-footed without a heel strike ("flat feet"). If you're interested in legal race walking, flap feet and flat feet can contribute to bent knees and, ultimately, might lead to a disqualification from a race. You might be walking this way subconsciously to avoid a shin ache because your lower legs are too weak to maintain or create a strong toe lift or heel strike. Or you might just be wearing very stiff shoes that don't allow you to roll through smoothly.

To strengthen your shins, try walking on your heels for a short distance as part of your warm-up or cooldown. Or try tapping your toes quickly, even while you're sitting at your desk. Perform either just until you can feel the front of your lower leg tire. Rest, then repeat several times.

Although it is the front of the lower leg that aches or is weak, remember you must strengthen the opposing muscle group, too. Incorporate heel raises into your warm-up or cooldown to strengthen your calves. Stand on a step or curb with your heels hanging off the edge. Start with your heels lower than the step, lift them high, then return to the starting position. Repeat 10 to 20 times, rest, and repeat.

You can also do ankle- and foot-strengthening exercises with rubber bands and weights, as described in several good exercise books. Yoga is great for strengthening neglected ankles, feet, and lower legs. And don't forget to stretch what you've strengthened.

Remember that the ache you might feel in your shin is probably not shin splints, but rather the complaint of an underused muscle that is suddenly being asked to perform. Just as your biceps might complain if you suddenly did 50 biceps curls when you usually do none, so will your shins complain if they're asked to do hundreds of toe lifts when they usually do few. Any minor ache can be relieved by an ice pack. However, if the ache continues for several hours after your walk, you might have an orthopedic problem that needs medical attention.

Learning proper walking technique at all levels is an ongoing task, but one well worth the effort because of the payback in performance and conditioning.

CHAPTER 4

WALKING WORKOUT DESIGN

Learning fast walking doesn't just mean walking as fast as you can every day. That's the way to get burned out and hurt, putting an end to any performance or conditioning goals you have.

Achieving greater fitness for increased performance means training your body's different energy systems by designing various workouts of distinct pace, distance, and effort or heart rate levels. Depending on your goal, your workout plan can include highly structured workouts of exactly measured distances at precise paces around a track or on a trail; less structured workouts on a trail or road that meet the same physiologic demands but are based on time and heart rate or perceived exertion; or completely unstructured workouts utilizing heart rate or perceived exertion based on the available terrain or environment.

Don't be shy to learn about and implement workouts with technical sounding names, such as "aerobic capacity," even if your goal isn't to be the speediest demon in the neighborhood. At whatever level and with whatever walking goal, the workouts in this chapter will help you get there quicker and add spice to your training program to keep you invigorated along the way.

Before you are able to plan your workouts, you need to know how to measure your exertion level using your heart rate and your perception of how hard you're working using Borg's Rating of Perceived Exertion, and understand how that relates to maximum oxygen consumption. Once you have that knowledge, I can discuss pace measurement. All of that will make you fully able to understand the pieces of a good training and conditioning program—the workouts themselves.

MEASURING INTENSITY

Without paying some attention to the intensity—or effort level—of a workout, exercisers tend to walk either too hard or too easy and not achieve the desired results. Highly competitive people tend to push too hard resulting in burnout or injury, while, without much prodding, less competitive types might poke along and not make training gains. I will briefly discuss three measures of intensity to help direct your workouts—the scientific $\dot{V}O_2$max, also known as maximum oxygen consumption, the easily measured (albeit somewhat error-prone unless you've been laboratory tested) percentages of heart rate maximum, and the feelings-based rating of perceived exertion that forces you to tune into your body. All vary depending on factors such as age, gender, training, and altitude.

Obviously, the intensity or effort level of your workout is usually correlated to the pace or speed of your walk. The faster you go, the more intense it becomes, and the slower you go, the less intense it becomes. But the true reading of your intensity is not in pace, but in the physiologic measures of maximum oxygen output and heart rate. There will be times when your intensity and effort are very high even though you are going slower than usual because you are tired, sick, or particularly stressed. Then there are those days when you seem to float through a workout, effortlessly gliding along faster than usual, but feeling as if you're hardly working. If only those workouts happened every day!

Along with recognizing what intensity is, you should also realize that the first couple of minutes of any moderate to hard workout will always feel easy—not very intense—because circulation and breathing take time to increase to aerobic levels. That means it's important to start sessions comfortably to let your body's engine warm up properly before you can accurately measure and perceive intensity.

No matter which measure of effort works for you, it's always important to listen to your body and not overjudge your capability. The goal is to choose an intensity that allows you to have a successful workout.

$\dot{V}O_2MAX$

Every body has a limit to its maximum ability to use oxygen, or $\dot{V}O_2$max. Much of this is determined genetically. Through training, you can increase your body's ability to transport and use oxygen, studies have shown, but only by about 5% to 15% greater. So even those gifted with a high $\dot{V}O_2$max must train diligently, especially training other energy systems, to realize their full potential (table 4.1).

Your $\dot{V}O_2$max is also limited by age, since research seems to indicate that it declines gradually after about your mid-20s. But more recent research also indicates that declines are not as dramatic as once thought if someone stays fit and athletic (Pollock, 1987). The 40-year-old Olympian isn't unusual these days. In addition to limits imposed by training and age, gender also puts bounds on $\dot{V}O_2$max; women's levels are lower because of their smaller body size, proportionately less muscle mass, and greater body fat.

The bottom line is, your $\dot{V}O_2$max is not the be-all, end-all measure of fitness that some like to tout because much of its determination is beyond your control. Nevertheless, it is interesting to note typical ranges of maximal oxygen consumption. Notice in table 4.1 how $\dot{V}O_2$max declines with age in the sedentary averages.

The few studies of $\dot{V}O_2$max in highly trained race walkers show that they have values comparable to other top-level athletes (Franklin, 1981).

Table 4.1 Comparisons of $\dot{V}O_2$max for Untrained and Trained Men and Women

	Women	Men
Sedentary, ages 20–29	33–42	43–52
Sedentary, ages 40–49	26–35	36–44
Speed skaters	44–53	56–73
Runners	50–75	60–85
Cross-country skiers	60–75	65–95
Swimmers	40–60	50–70

Note: Measures are in milliliters per kilogram per minute (ml/kg/min).
Adapted from Wilmore and Costill, 1994.

If you want to know your $\dot{V}O_2$max—either for more scientifically based training or out of curiosity—some community colleges and universities have exercise testing classes open to the public, or may need guinea pigs for student-run research projects. Some high-end health clubs might also have appropriate facilities, and some metropolitan areas have athletic performance laboratories that specialize in testing. A test will typically involve a progressive treadmill run that starts with an easy walk with no grade and graduates to a fast run on a steep grade.

Remember, however, that several things can influence the accuracy of your results. For example, expect lower maximal readings if you aren't properly rested or are at altitude. In addition, studies show that a person will be able to produce a higher reading if they are tested doing an activity in which they are trained. In other words, best readings occur when runners run, skaters skate, or walkers walk. (There are protocols to test walkers while walking, but these aren't commonly known.) Last, never forget that your evaluation results are only as good as the evaluator.

If you're a numbers maniac and want to know yours, look in the telephone book, call local colleges, or ask at area athletic stores to find out where you can get tested.

HEART RATE

Maximum heart rates, upon which target training ranges or zones are based to develop the body's different energy systems, can be calculated using a simplified version of a well-known formula. The problem is, that like $\dot{V}O_2$max, a person's maximum heart rate is genetic and can vary by up to 15 beats per minute, more or less. So although most of us use the age-graded heart rate formula—and so will I in this book—understand that it is merely a starting point. It takes several months to really get to know your body and to personalize your heart rate–based training.

For example, if the formula says you must train between heart rates X and Y for a "comfortably hard" workout, and you're barely breathing hard, after a few weeks you might want to try something a little more intense. Or, if the formula says working between heart rates X and Y will be easy but you're panting and dragging, your true maximum heart rate might require you to shift the percentages downward.

I know athletes whose maximums are so high that the formula would tell them their hearts are about to explode. I know another

50-something man who can do extended, comfortably hard workouts at a heart rate that should be above his age-based maximum.

Nevertheless, you need to start somewhere. Thus, calculate your maximum and your target zones based on these formulas.

If you're a man, subtract your age from 220 (220 – age = maximum heart rate), then multiply the resulting maximum by your selected intensity (percent of max HR) to determine your target zones. For example, a 45-year-old man would do the following:

$$220 - 45 = 175 \text{ (max HR)}$$

$175 \times .69 = 121$ (easy workout at 69% of max HR) $175 \times .80 = 140$ (threshold workout at 80% of max HR)

Women use a similar formula, substituting 226 for 220, since women's hearts are smaller and tend to beat slightly faster. For example, a 30-year-old woman would do the following:

$$226 - 30 = 196 \text{ (max HR)}$$

$196 \times .69 = 135$ (easy workout at 69% of max HR) $196 \times .80 = 157$ (threshold workout at 80% of max HR)

Refer to tables 4.2 and 4.3 for calculations of heart rates of different intensities for men and women ages 20 to 75.

A wireless heart rate monitor can be an invaluable tool for safe and effective training. These devices, which work like electrocardiograms in hospitals, eliminate not only the need to stop, feel for a pulse, and count, but also the margin of human error. You simply strap on a chest belt that picks up the electrical signals produced by your heart, and a wrist receiver that looks like a watch and continuously shows a precise heart rate reading. That way, an occasional glance during a workout alerts you to your intensity and allows you to modify up or down.

Since calculating heart rate ranges and monitoring pulses are within the grasp of everyone, I will primarily use this method to rank workouts and training programs, as well as to keep us smart about getting enough rest. In a later section of this chapter, I will discuss the pulse ranges of various types of workouts and their physiological basis so you can properly build a walking program.

Table 4.2 Age-Based Heart Rates for Men, Ages 20–75

AGE						
% max HR	20	25	30	35	40	45
100	200	195	190	185	180	175
90	180	176	171	167	162	158
80	160	156	152	148	144	140
70	140	137	133	130	126	123
60	120	117	114	111	108	105
50	100	98	95	93	90	88
% max HR	50	55	60	65	70	75
100	170	165	160	155	150	145
90	153	149	144	140	135	131
80	136	132	128	124	120	116
70	119	116	112	109	105	102
60	102	99	96	93	90	87
50	85	83	80	78	75	73

RATING OF PERCEIVED EXERTION

The Rating of Perceived Exertion, or RPE, may complement heart rate monitoring in deciding appropriate workout ranges. As I stated, heart rate maximums vary widely based on genetics, so you will use the perception of your exertion level to gauge the correctness of your calculated heart rates. Once you fine-tune your ability to mentally calculate your exertion, you will find yourself combining the two methods regularly to hit upon the best place for your workouts.

Discovering perceived exertion forces you to tune in to your body, an important concept in any training and conditioning program. Your

Table 4.3 Age-Based Heart Rates for Women, Ages 20–75						
AGE						
% max HR	**20**	**25**	**30**	**35**	**40**	**45**
100	206	201	196	191	186	181
90	185	181	176	172	167	163
80	165	161	157	153	149	145
70	144	141	137	134	130	123
60	124	121	118	115	112	106
50	103	101	98	96	93	88
% max HR	**50**	**55**	**60**	**65**	**70**	**75**
100	176	171	166	161	156	151
90	158	154	149	145	140	136
80	141	137	133	129	125	121
70	123	120	116	113	109	106
60	106	103	100	97	94	91
50	88	86	83	81	78	76

body is very intelligent and, if given the chance, will clue you in to all kinds of things going on, be it mental stress, overtraining, or an impending illness.

The RPE was developed initially in the 1960s by Dr. Gunnar Borg using a scale of 6 to 20, which researchers found corresponded very closely to heart rates if you added a zero to the RPE. But the public found rating themselves on such an odd numeric scale rather cumbersome. So, two decades later, Borg came up with a modified 0 to 10 scale that incorporates words to describe each level (table 4.4).

Table 4.4	Rating of Perceived Exertion (RPE) Scale	
0	Nothing at all
0.5	Extremely weak (just noticeable)
1	Very weak
2	Weak (light)
3	Moderate
4	
5	Strong (heavy)
6	
7	Very strong
8	
9	
10	Extremely strong (almost max)
•	Maximal

Reprinted from Borg 1982. © Gunnar Borg, 1981, 1982.

MEASURING PACE

Those of you who don't care for much structure can choose workouts based on time and exertion level rather than distance, or even completely unstructured workouts we'll discuss later, so you won't care about measuring your speed. Some of you, however, will want to know exactly how fast and far you're going. I encourage you, though, to choose some workouts based strictly on time and effort in order to occasionally dislodge your eyes from the watch and help you tune in to your body.

Obviously, the most common way to calculate pace is to time how long it takes to cover the measured distance from point A to point B. But there are other ways, too.

TRAILS AND ROADS

Some cities have recreation trails that are measured and marked every quarter or half mile, making it easy to know how far you've gone and to time yourself. You can also drive a route you commonly walk and estimate how far it is, although exact distances are difficult to measure because of the error factor in a car's odometer.

TRACKS

Going to a school, community, or health club track is one solution. This is desirable for some exact workouts or for personal safety, since you'll know you'll be around other people. Know that a track's first lane is commonly either 440 yards (a quarter mile) or 400 meters (2.3 meters short of a quarter mile), with each lane outward adding approximately 7 to 7.5 yards (6.5 to 7 meters) per lap. For example, covering 1 1/2 miles in the outside lane might only take approximately 5 1/2 laps instead of 6.

Some indoor facilities and health clubs have odd-sized tracks that require anywhere from 8 to 16 laps for a mile. At those facilities, signs will usually be posted explaining the distance as well as the directional etiquette. They might ask patrons to go clockwise on Tuesday, Thursday, and Saturday, and counterclockwise on other days. Continually turning in one direction, especially on tighter tracks, can put imbalanced strain on your soft tissues.

STEPS PER MINUTE

This method (see table 4.5) comes in handy, especially if you're curious how fast you're going while walking an unmarked route such as unfamiliar roads or trails when you travel. This is only an estimate, since stride lengths vary, not only from walker to walker, but from slow to fast. For example, as you get faster, your stride length will increase slightly without losing the turnover and without overstriding. It is best to count your steps per minute (count one leg and multiply by two) at various speeds on several occasions when you walk a marked distance, then come up with your personal average. When in unmarked areas, you then count your

Track and Trail Etiquette

Know how to share the outdoors with fellow exercisers to keep everyone happy, healthy, and injury-free:

1. The first two lanes on a track are reserved for walkers or runners of any speed doing timed interval workouts. If you are warming up, cooling down, or just walking without regard to your time per lap, stick to lanes 6, 7, or 8.

2. Avoid walking side by side with other walkers in the first lane of a track because it makes it more difficult for faster exercisers to pass.

3. As soon as you finish your interval in the first lane, step quickly out of the way or off the track. Someone might be coming behind you.

4. Treat tracks and trails like roads: Look both ways before entering to avoid accidents.

5. On recreational trails, walk to the right and avoid walking in packs so there is room to your left for others on foot or on wheels to pass.

6. If you're passing someone on a trail, call out "On your left" as an advance warning so you don't startle the person.

7. On a track, if you are doing a timed interval, walk a straight line. That way someone faster will be able to judge where you will be and can pass safely.

8. If you forget to stay clear of the first two lanes of the track on casual walks or while warming up and someone yells "Track please" or "Lane please," move immediately out of the way.

9. Trails are for moving, so do any socializing, stretching, or resting on the side, not in the middle.

10. If you spit during workouts, look before you let it go.

11. Leave perfume, aftershave, or cologne at home. Sweat intensifies the odors to annoying or even asthma-inducing levels.

12. Smoking anything, anywhere near a track or trail where people are exercising is ignorant.

steps to get an idea of your pace. Or you can translate into miles per hour if you're on a treadmill.

MENU OF WORKOUTS

Developing workouts for fast walking has always presented walkers and their coaches with a real challenge. Research in training physiology rarely involves fast walkers, instead focusing on runners, cyclists, or swimmers. Often, studies that do involve walkers have one of three drawbacks for our purposes: looking at low-speed walking and basic health benefits or weight loss rather than performance; analyzing biomechanics of elite race walkers; or using runners or inexperienced walkers and asking them to walk fast without technique training.

Table 4.5	Estimating Your Pace With Steps per Minute	
Steps/min	**MPH**	**Min/mile**
60–80	2.0–2.4	25–30
85–95	2.5–2.9	21–24
100–115	3.0–3.3	18–20
120–125	3.4–3.6	16:30–17:30
130–135	3.8–4.0	15–16
140–145	4.3–4.6	13–14
150–155	4.6–4.8	12:30–13
160–165	5.0–5.2	11:30–12
170–175	5.5–5.7	10:30–11
180–185	6.5–6.7	9–9:15
190–195	7.0–7.2	8:15–8:30
>195	>7.5	>8

Note that your actual speed and steps will vary depending on technique, terrain, and leg length.

Adapted from Iknoian 1995.

Therefore, workouts for walkers are rather loosely based on the physiology of training used by runners and decades of trial and error in the walking community. Obviously, the basic energy systems used by runners and walkers—or any endurance athletes—are the same. But biomechanical and technical differences between running and walking involving stride rate, technique demands, upper-body use, and turnover versus speed make direct translations difficult and complex.

If you become confused by trying to take concepts presented in a training book for runners or other endurance athletes to develop ideas for your own walking workouts, remember one piece of advice: Translate workouts and training programs by time, not by distance. For example, if you are training for a 10-kilometer distance (with times from 40 to 50 minutes all the way to 75 to 85 minutes), you would find better results following workouts aimed at a runner training for a half marathon (13.1 miles) because completion times are comparable. For example, if a runner's workout talks of repeat 880s (half miles or two track laps), you would be better to consider repeat 440s (quarter miles or one track lap) or 660s (one and a half track laps) depending on the runner's speed, calculating comparable percentages of rest.

Following are five different types of workouts. I will explain the basic goal of each, as well as how to develop each one to suit your performance and conditioning needs, and how to determine your pace and ratios for each. I will also provide examples of how each might be designed as a highly structured, moderately structured, or unstructured workout.

First, some definitions:

- **Intervals**—Periods of walking and resting within one workout, rather than moving at a steady pace. Intervals can be long (15 or 20 minutes) or short (30 to 90 seconds), but are always separated by rest periods.
- **Work**—The time between your rest breaks when you're exercising harder, therefore raising your heart rate.
- **Rest**—The time between your work periods, when you move easily to allow your body to recover (for example, your heart rate slows) so you can do another walking work interval. Length varies based on physiologic goals and the speed of the interval. You might choose "half rest" (half the length of the preceding work interval), "equal rest" (equal to the length of the preceding work interval), or "double rest" (double the length).

- **Ratio**—The relationship in an interval workout between work and rest; 1:3, for example, means 1 minute of work for every 3 minutes of rest.
- **Set**—The combination of one work period and one rest period.
- **Aerobic**—Working with oxygen. Your body can make enough oxygen to keep up with the supply needed for your muscles.
- **Anaerobic**—Working without oxygen. Your body can't keep up with the demand for oxygen.
- **Anaerobic threshold**—The zone between aerobic work and anaerobic work when your body begins to demand more oxygen than can be supplied and begins to produce an excess of waste products, including lactic acid. Also called lactate threshold and, more technically, OBLA (onset of blood lactate accumulation), since the blood is where the lactic acid, or lactate, builds up.

With this in mind, I can briefly discuss the workout menu, starting at the lowest effort. Refer to table 4.6 as you read for a comparison of efforts. Note that novice walkers should do workouts at the lower end of the effort range for each workout type, while more experienced walkers might want to push toward the higher end.

EASY

This is exactly as its name says, with the goal to allow muscles to adapt to walking's biomechanics. Easy workouts will allow you to rest and recover between harder workouts and are one of the best times to practice technique, since you're going slowly enough to concentrate on your movement. You might hear the term "garbage" miles or "junk" miles for workouts that are just easy. I don't agree—as long as you don't ignore your technique and continue to think about how you're moving. Anytime you're on your feet moving forward, you are strengthening your body and conditioning your cardiovascular system. Think of these as "technique" miles, since they are slow enough for you to focus on correcting yourself and are an opportunity to try some drills.

The effort should be a steady pace, guilt-producingly comfortable and extremely conversational; your heart rate should stay low—about 55% to 69% of maximum, or an RPE of about 1 to 3. These can be measured based on distance (for example, 3 to 4 miles) or time (30 to 60 minutes).

Table 4.6   Workout Effort Comparisons

	% $\dot{V}O_2$ max	% max HR	Rating of perceived exertion	Feeling of effort
Easy	35–55	55–69	1–3 Very easy to easy	Very comfortable, extremely light effort
Long	50–65	60–74	2–4 Fairly easy to somewhat hard	Conversational, mostly comfortable
Anaerobic threshold	65–85	75–89	5–7 Somewhat hard to hard	Comfortably hard; can speak brief phrases; can't converse
Aerobic capacity	85–90	90–94	8 Hard to very hard	High breathing rate; prefer not to talk
Anaerobic capacity	90–110+	95–100+	9–10+ Very, very hard to maximal	Feel muscular fatigue; heart is pounding when done

LONG

These workouts allow your body to develop aerobic endurance, while also strengthening soft tissues such as muscles and tendons to prepare them for faster workouts.

The effort should also be steady, fairly comfortable, and still conversational. Heart rates may be as low as 60% up to a high of about 74%, or an RPE of about 2 to 4. More experienced walkers familiar with their race paces might do these as fast as 1 1/2 to 2 minutes or so slower than the per-mile pace needed to complete a 10-kilometer race. Beginners, however, are advised to keep these workouts on the less-intense side, like extended easy walks, concentrating instead on completing the distance. Long workouts are a great time to socialize with fellow walkers, especially since company can make the time fly on walks of 60 to more than 120 minutes. Don't be deceived by the low effort level of long walks; it is the length that makes them a developmental stress on the body.

These can also be measured based on distance or time. In some cases, you can also break up the mileage; instead of doing 10 continuous miles, you can do 5 miles in the morning and 5 miles in the evening.

ANAEROBIC THRESHOLD

For most walkers, these workouts are the foundation of a good training program, allowing you to push your body's endurance and speed by raising your threshold. What that means is you'll be able to go faster while staying aerobic and not developing excess amounts of waste products that make you slow down. Developing your threshold is one of the most important ways to improve your performance and condition. Note that a high $\dot{V}O_2$max will do you little good unless your threshold isn't pushed upward (see figure 4.1).

Monitor your efforts carefully, be astute about not working out too hard. RPEs will be in the range of 5 to 7, corresponding with heart rates of about 75% to 89%. If you are a novice walker you will find you must keep these workouts closer to 75% or 80%; as an intermediate exerciser, you may maintain a pulse in the low- to mid-80% range; strong

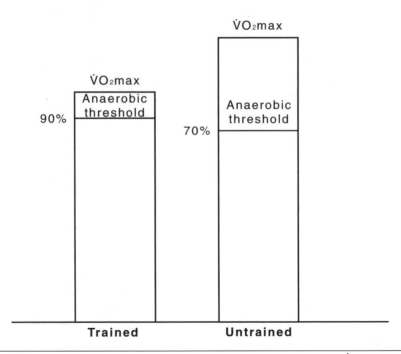

Figure 4.1 Note how an untrained person with a genetically high $\dot{V}O_2$max might have an anaerobic threshold that is lower than a trained person with a genetically lower maximal oxygen consumption.

athletes may push toward 90%. Note that national- and international-class endurance athletes have shown thresholds in the high 90s! You should feel as if these workouts are comfortably hard. Although you can't hold a nonstop conversation or sing, you should be able to speak brief phrases. Less experienced walkers may find this pace corresponds to, or is slightly slower than, their 1-mile walk time from chapter 2.

Threshold workouts may be done either as longer intervals with less structure based on time (for example, 5 to 20 minutes) or using more structured distance (half mile to 2 miles), with easy walking between each interval. They may also be done as a steady workout of 15 to 40 continuous minutes at the lower end of the threshold intensity range. You might hear these called "tempo" workouts.

AEROBIC CAPACITY

These are longer intervals that will improve your body's $\dot{V}O_2$max. With an improved $\dot{V}O_2$max, you'll be able to use oxygen more efficiently and improve your speed.

Your effort in aerobic capacity workouts will be hard to very hard, or an RPE of about 8, with a high rate of breathing. You will prefer not to talk. Remember that these hard bursts are done with a good amount of rest in between so they aren't so daunting or overly exhausting. Your heart rate will reach 90% to 94% of its maximum depending on the length of the interval. As you get more fit, the longer it takes your heart rate to reach its maximum for the workout; so in shorter aerobic-capacity intervals you will likely not see a number that corresponds to the above percentages, but a number that would reach that peak if the effort were to be longer. You will soon learn about how high that number is for you and will be able to gauge your workouts relatively. Here, RPE can serve well after the first 2 minutes. More experienced walkers could have reached this pace in the 1-mile test.

These intervals can be done in many ways on the road, trail, or track, or using different terrain or environments. Whatever method, they will usually be 4 to 6 minutes long—sometimes as short as 3 minutes—with a maximum length of 8 or 9 minutes. Each is followed by a rest period equal to the work (1:1). If performing them in a structured track setting, you can do identical distances and exactly time the rest. If on the road or trail, you can alternate hard and easy periods (called "fartlek," which is Swedish for speed play), doing a certain length of time at a certain RPE, then easing off. If in a hilly area, you can go hard up the hill (if it's long enough) and go easier, even jogging, on the way down. Or you can use urban landmarks, going hard for a certain number of telephone poles or garbage cans, before easing back to recover.

ANAEROBIC CAPACITY

These workouts serve to improve your speed, leg turnover, and biomechanical efficiency or style. Improved biomechanics lead to less wasted energy and better performance.

The effort of these short bursts is more difficult to quantify, since they are basically too short to begin to feel really strenuous. Although classified as a 9 to 10 or greater RPE—or very, very hard to maximal—with heart rates reaching 95% to 100% or more, your heart rate usually can't reach that level during the short work period, especially if you're more fit. More likely, you will feel muscular fatigue, a heaviness in your legs, which will progress to a cumulative cardiovascular fatigue toward the end of several sets of anaerobic capacity intervals. Another common feeling is a pounding heart as soon as you stop. Because of the high muscular demands, in order to avoid injury it is important for someone to have a strong aerobic base and good muscular conditioning before trying these.

Since these are so intense with a goal of good technique, the work periods are only 30 seconds to 2 minutes, with the amount of rest double to triple (1:2 or 1:3) that of the preceding work. Like aerobic capacity intervals, these can be done either more structured on the track, or as speed play on the road or trail. Try the track, too, for a less-structured version, going hard on the straights and easy on the turns, or some combination thereof. With such short work periods, anaerobic-capacity fartlek can really liven up a workout on a trail and make for fun competition with yourself and others.

In the next chapter, you will see samples of each type of workout, including structured and unstructured versions, and ones based on time or distance. These will help you fully understand the physiologic and conditioning concepts so you'll be better able to develop your own walking workouts.

Chapter 5

Sample Walking Workouts

This chapter's workouts are an attempt to illustrate several examples of each type of training walk explained previously. I've compiled a broad range of possible walks. Put together, they fulfill the requirements of easy workouts to anaerobic capacity workouts for all fitness levels and for whatever goal you might have. Included are structured, as well as unstructured, walks that can serve as templates to help you design your own walking workouts for your personal needs, schedule, and level of commitment.

Obviously, it is possible to simply use these as presented in this chapter week after week, month after month. Some of you will likely do that, too, but I don't recommend it after the initial stage of trying them out. Simply referring to these workout after workout not only would be monotonous, but also would cheat you out of the opportunity to mold workouts to suit your tastes. Additionally, only using these could under- or overtrain you, since they are designed only as examples and might not fit your personal mileage or effort needs.

Here's what you should do, after understanding the basic guidelines for effort and heart rate (summarized in table 4.6) and workout speed or length established in the previous chapter:

1. Read the workouts in this chapter, cross-referencing their design with those guidelines to understand their development.

2. Try one or more of each type as a part of your program to understand how each type feels. (Of course, you should shorten or lengthen them to accommodate your program's mileage percentages, as explained in chapter 4.)

3. Write one of your own of each kind, using a sample as a template. Table 4.6 can help you do this.

Soon, you'll be your own coach extraordinaire, coming up with great workouts to suit your needs and taste. Use your imagination and creativity because designing workouts is a lot like cooking a gourmet soup—one week you'll throw in leeks and chicken, the next week you might prefer potatoes and green chilies, the following week you opt for noodles and carrots.

Don't get so stuck in a rut that you can't go a different way on a trail, add double-backs, or modify what you've planned on a moment's notice based on your schedule, the weather, or the terrain. This is especially true if you travel. It's not been unusual for me to get to a city, knowing I've planned a workout of a certain time and length, only to discover that it's snowing, I'm surrounded by hills, the track is closed, or any number of other unimagined confounding variables. Be flexible.

If structured workouts—even occasionally—suit your fancy, you might want to find a recreation trail or park path in your city that is marked in quarter or half miles. Actually, this is not unusual, especially in outdoorsy or athletically-oriented urban areas, such as Indianapolis, Indiana; San Diego, California; Aspen, Colorado; or Spokane, Washington. Often, if you pay attention to the ground under your feet, you'll discover some running club has been there before you and has spray-painted distance markings on the side of the trail, or a local race uses the area and has marked every mile. If you aren't sure where marked trails in your area are, contact a local running or walking club, or a technical (not a chain) athletic store where there are usually people who know where to head for workouts.

One warning: Always be skeptical of the accuracy of any markings, especially if you find your time by these markings is suddenly a lot faster or a lot slower than usual. With experience, you'll be able to guesstimate within a few feet the distance you've walked because you'll be so well-acquainted with your body's sensations at different intensities.

Other venues suitable for workouts include park roads, trimmed but grassy athletic fields (hopefully with level dirt underneath the grass), college campus paths, business or industrial parks or access roads (often traffic free after hours), covered parking garages (in bad weather), or even malls in early mornings (many open early for walkers). Because of walking's emphasis on technique, low leg swing, and heel plant, you'll likely find it an annoying disturbance to your rhythm and pace if you have to dodge pedestrians on sidewalks, jump curbs, or stop for traffic.

If nothing in your area is marked for distance except local school tracks, borrow or rent a surveyor's wheel, get a can of marking paint from a hardware store, and go to it. Mark whatever increments suit your fancy. Other area walkers and runners will probably appreciate your efforts!

For the following workout samples, I've gone on the premise that you've been walking for at least 4 months and perhaps as long as a year, putting in a minimum of 3 to 4 days a week, 3 to 4 miles each day, totaling a good weekly foundation of 10 to 15 miles on which you can now build. You're probably already able to do at least a 14- or 15-minute mile without straining, and perhaps even a 12-minute mile isn't that difficult for you. If you haven't been walking that long or that often, take at least 6 to 12 weeks of easy to long workouts only, without worrying about speed, to establish some base conditioning, endurance, and walking strength. If you aren't as speedy as 15-minute miles, simply adjust workouts slower to suit your ability.

Based on that assumption, I've designed these sample workouts for an imaginary walker who will train at least 3 to 5 days a week, covering 4 to 6 miles each time, for a weekly total of 12 to 30 miles. You'll probably be doing these workouts at a 10- to 15-minute mile pace . . . or perhaps faster!

Remember that these workouts do not include the details of a warm-up or cooldown. Both are mandatory, except in easy or long workouts where the first few minutes can serve as a warm-up and the last few minutes can be your cooldown. To read more about the specifics of warming up and cooling down, as well as suggestions on how to construct them, refer to the section on how to stay injury free in chapter 6.

You'll find each workout presented individually, with comments as needed to explain a concept or location. Then you'll find all the workouts of each type summarized in a table for easier comparison and referral (see tables 5.1 through 5.5). Study these, tear them apart, understand their concepts, then use what you've learned to develop your own.

EASY WORKOUTS

Easy Workout 1—Unstructured

Measurement: Time

Length: 35 minutes

Effort: 55%–69% max HR; RPE 1–3

Rest: None; continuous walk

Location: Any suitable or convenient road, trail, or track

Comments: Don't worry about distance; just walk the needed time for your program at the appropriate effort. You could cover 2 to 3 1/2 miles, depending on your pace.

Easy Workout 2—Unstructured

Measurement: Time

Length: 50 minutes

Effort: 55%–69% max HR; RPE 1–3

Rest: None; continuous walk

Location: Any suitable or convenient road, trail, or track

Comments: Only the time on your feet at the appropriate effort, not distance, is a concern. This one is longer, if you are doing a few more miles, allowing you to walk from 3 to 5 miles.

Easy Workout 3—Structured

Measurement: Distance

Length: 3 miles

Effort: 55%–69% max HR; RPE 1–3

Rest: None; continuous walk

Location: Any trail, track, or road marked for distance; remember if you walk in an outside track lane, you'll cover more distance (up to 50 or 60 meters) per lap

Comments: Keep this at the right effort as you cover the distance. You might need 30 to 45 minutes to do this.

Easy Workout 4—Structured

Measurement: Distance

Length: 4 1/2 miles

Effort: 55%–69% max HR; RPE 1–3

Rest: None; continuous walk

Location: Any that is accurately marked, even if you just drive a street in your car for an approximate distance

Comments: This could take you 45 to 67 minutes, not including stretching time.

Table 5.1 Easy Workouts Summary
Effort: 55%–69% max HR, RPE 1–3

Workout	Type	Measurement	Length	Rest	Location
1	Unstructured	Time	35 min	None	Road, trail, or track
2	Unstructured	Time	50 min	None	Road, trail, or track
3	Structured	Distance	3 mi	None	Road, trail, or track
4	Structured	Distance	4 1/2 mi	None	Road, trail, or track

LONG WORKOUTS

Long Workout 1—Unstructured

Measurement: Time

Length: 60 minutes

Effort: 60%–74% max HR; RPE 2–4

Rest: None; continuous walk

Location: Any suitable road or trail, perhaps slightly rolling

Comments: Stay on your feet an hour, during which time you'll cover 4 to 6 miles. This is a good long workout for you if your normal walks are 3 to 4 miles.

Long Workout 2—Unstructured

Measurement: Time

Length: 90 minutes

Effort: 60%–74% max HR; RPE 2–4

Rest: None; continuous walk

Location: Any suitable road, park path, or trail

Comments: Keep the pace steady and you'll cover 6 to 9 miles, a good long workout for you if your weekly mileage reaches 20 to 30 miles.

Long Workout 3—Structured

Measurement: Distance

Length: 6 miles

Effort: 60%–74% max HR; RPE 2–4

Rest: None; continuous walk

Location: Any convenient trail or path; add hills if desired

Comments: For you if you like to count miles. This will take 60 to 90 minutes and is good for you if you are doing 20 to 30 miles weekly.

Long Workout 4—Structured

Measurement: Distance

Length: 10 miles

Effort: 60%–74% max HR; RPE 2–4

Rest: None; continuous walk

Location: Any marked trail or a convenient road

Comments: Try this only if you're regularly covering at least 30 miles a week. It will take you 1 hour and 40 minutes to 2 1/2 hours!

Long Workout 5—Structured

Measurement: Distance

Length: 10 miles, broken into two 5-mile workouts

Effort: 60–74% max HR; RPE 2–4

Rest: 4–8 hours between walks

Location: Any marked trail or a convenient road

Comments: Split up your long workout day into two shorter segments if you don't have time to do it all at once. Each walk will take 50 to 75 minutes at a steady 10- to 15-minute mile pace.

Table 5.2 Long Workouts Summary
Effort: 60%–74% max HR, RPE 2–4

Workout	Type	Measurement	Length	Rest	Location
1	Unstructured	Time	60 min	None	Road or trail
2	Unstructured	Time	90 min	None	Road, path, or trail
3	Structured	Distance	6 mi	None	Path or trail
4	Structured	Distance	10 mi	None	Road or trail
5	Structured	Distance	2 × 5 mi	4–8 h	Road or trail

ANAEROBIC THRESHOLD WORKOUTS

Anaerobic Threshold Workout 1— Unstructured/Interval

Measurement: Time

Length: 30 minutes, broken into two 15-minute segments

Effort: 75%–89% max HR; RPE 5–7

Rest: 4 minutes

Location: A paved, fairly flat trail or road

Comments: These shouldn't be too easy, but should fall into the "comfortably hard" range of workouts. Lengthen the rest by 30 seconds if you're very tired at the end of the first segment.

Anaerobic Threshold Workout 2— Unstructured/Interval

Measurement: Time or landmarks

Length: 30 minutes, broken into five 6-minute segments

Effort: 75%–89% max HR; RPE 5–7

Rest: 75–110 seconds between segments

Location: A paved, smooth, flat surface

Comments: Note how you can break down the total workout time further compared to Workout 1, with rest periods shortened since each work period is shorter. If using landmark measurement, go harder around one block, for example, then easy for half a block and repeat; or go hard for six telephone poles, then easy for two. Also try three 10-minute segments, or four at 8 minutes.

Anaerobic Threshold Workout 3— Structured/Interval

Measurement: Distance

Length: 2 1/2 miles, broken into two 1 1/4 mile segments

Effort: 75%–89% max HR; RPE 5–7

Rest: A fifth to a third of the time it took you to complete the first interval

Location: Track or marked trail

Comments: This is comparable to Anaerobic Threshold Workout 1, but using distance.

Anaerobic Threshold Workout 4— Structured/Interval

Measurement: Distance

Length: 2 1/2 miles, broken into half-mile segments

Effort: 75%–89% max HR; RPE 5–7

Rest: One-fifth the time it takes you to complete each segment, or as little as 60 seconds, up to perhaps 90 seconds

Location: Track or marked trail

Comments: Notice that the rest leans toward the short end of the range as the work intervals get shorter.

Anaerobic Threshold Workout 5— Unstructured/Continuous

Measurement: Time

Length: 25 minutes

Effort: 75%–84% max HR; RPE 5–6. Remember, use a slightly lower intensity since you are not taking rests.

Rest: None; continuous "tempo" walk

Location: Any convenient path or trail

Comments: Keep your effort on the lower end of the threshold range and walk steadily without a recovery break, covering 1 1/2 to 2 1/2 miles. These continuous threshold workouts (workouts 5, 6, and 7) are called "tempo" walks.

Anaerobic Threshold Workout 6— Structured/Continuous

Measurement: Distance

Length: 3 miles

Effort: 75%–84% max HR; RPE 5–6

Rest: None; continuous "tempo" walk

Location: A local trail marked for distance or an area track

Comments: This is another version of a continuous threshold workout (as are workouts 5 and 7), this time using miles. Try this distance if you're covering at least 22 miles weekly.

Anaerobic Threshold Workout 7—Structured/Interval

Measurement: Distance

Length: 2 1/2–3 miles, broken into quarter miles

Effort: 75%–84% max HR; RPE 5–6

Rest: 15–25 seconds between quarter miles

Location: Local track or marked trail

Comments: This is a good alternative to Threshold Workouts 5 and 6. Although intervals, the rests are so short that your heart rate hardly drops, making this more similar to a continuous workout. The rest gives your leg muscles a few seconds to recover so you can continue strongly. It's also a good way to stay mentally alert, since you're continually stopping and starting. Do this as an alternative or use it more often if you find you get bored by the continuous tempo walk.

Table 5.3 Anaerobic Threshold Workouts Summary
Effort: 75%–89% max HR, RPE 5–7

Workout	Type	Measurement	Length	Rest	Location
1	Unstructured/ interval	Time	2 × 15 min	4 min	Trail or road
2	Unstructured/ interval	Time or landmarks	5 × 6 min	1:15– 1:50 min	Track or marked trail
3	Structured/ interval	Distance	2 × 1 1/4 mi	20%	Track or marked trail
4	Structured/ interval	Distance	5 × 800 m	20%–30%	Trail or road
5	Unstructured/ continuous	Time	25 min	None	Trail or road
6	Structured/ continuous	Distance	3 mi	None	Trail, road, or track
7	Structured/ interval	Distance	10–12 × 400 m	15–25 s	Track or marked trail

AEROBIC CAPACITY WORKOUTS

Aerobic Capacity Workout 1—Unstructured

Measurement: Time or landmarks

Length: 16 minutes, broken into four 4-minute segments

Effort: 90%–94% max HR; RPE 8

Rest: 4 minutes, or equal to the work interval

Location: Any smooth, paved surface

Comments: Either use time and effort to walk hard for 4 minutes and easy for 4; or use landmarks to walk hard for part of a block or a certain number of driveways or trees, then easy for the same time. Repeat the same time or landmark measure.

Aerobic Capacity Workout 2—Unstructured

Measurement: Time or landmarks

Length: 15 minutes, broken into three 5-minute segments

Effort: 90%–94% max HR; RPE 8

Rest: 5 minutes, or equal to the work interval

Location: Any smooth, paved surface

Comments: This is another variation of the first aerobic capacity workout, using the same concepts of time and landmarks for measurement. It can be helpful to pick a distance on the first interval that you can cover in about the planned time, then just repeat that distance each time for a relative comparison. You'll probably cover 1 to 1 1/2 miles.

Aerobic Capacity Workout 3—Structured

Measurement: Time

Length: 18 minutes, constructed like a short pyramid with intervals of 4 minutes, 5 minutes, 5 minutes, then finishing with 4 minutes again

Effort: 90%–94% max HR; RPE 8

Rest: 4–5 minutes, or equal to the preceding work interval

Location: Any convenient trail, park path, or street

Comments: Note how the "pyramid" ascends, then descends. You can use this idea to construct many imaginative pyramid workouts. Try shorter times too (for example, 2 minutes, 3 minutes, 4 minutes, then back down 3 and 2, with rests equal to the previous work interval).

Aerobic Capacity Workout 4—Structured

Measurement: Time

Length: 18 minutes, in a descending ladder of 7 minutes, 6 minutes, then 5 minutes

Effort: 90%–94% max HR; RPE 8

Rest: 6–7 minutes, or equal to the preceding work interval

Location: Any convenient trail, street, or path

Comments: A ladder can be another fun way to structure interval workouts—either descending like this one or ascending, such as 4 minutes, 6 minutes, then 8 minutes. Just walk hard for the work time of each interval, then walk easy for the rest time.

Aerobic Capacity Workout 5—Structured

Measurement: Distance

Length: 1 1/2 miles, broken into three intervals in a descending ladder of 1 kilometer (2 1/2 laps), 800 meters (or two laps) and 600 meters (or 1 1/2 laps)

Effort: 90%–94% max HR; RPE 8

Rest: Equal to the time it takes you to complete the preceding work interval

Location: School track

Comments: For distances like this, it doesn't really matter if the track you choose is 400 meters or 440 yards. Just do the appointed laps and call it close enough. You'll only be a split second off.

Aerobic Capacity Workout 6—Structured

Measurement: Distance

Length: 3,000 meters (1.86 miles), broken into five 600-meter (1 1/2-lap) intervals

Effort: 90%–94% max HR; RPE 8

Rest: Equal to the work period (probably 4–5 minutes or slightly faster)

Location: School track

Comments: Sometimes just doing a straightforward session of "repeats" (one distance, repeated for the allotted length) can be a mindless change of pace from ladders and pyramids, while serving the same function.

Table 5.4   Aerobic Capacity Workouts Summary
Effort: 90%–94% max HR, RPE 8

Workout	Type	Measurement	Length	Rest	Location
1	Unstructured	Time or landmarks	4 × 4 min	4 min	Road or trail
2	Unstructured	Time or landmarks	3 × 5 min	5 min	Road or trail
3	Structured	Time	4-5-5-4 min	4–5 min	Road or trail
4	Structured	Time	7-6-5 min	6–7 min	Road or trail
5	Structured	Distance	1K-800 m-600 m	Equal	Track
6	Structured	Distance	5 × 600 m	Equal	Track

ANAEROBIC CAPACITY WORKOUTS

Anaerobic Capacity Workout 1—Unstructured

Measurement: Time or landmarks

Length: 6 minutes, broken into four 1 1/2-minute intervals

Effort: 95%–100% max HR; RPE 9–10

Rest: 3–4 minutes

Location: Any road, trail, or street free from traffic

Comments: Like the unstructured aerobic capacity workouts, these can be done with one eye on the watch, or you can use landmarks, such as residential blocks, telephone poles, or driveways. Another option: Do each 1 1/2-minute work interval up a moderate incline, then use the rest to walk easily back down.

Anaerobic Capacity Workout 2—Unstructured

Measurement: Time or landmarks

Length: 7 1/2 minutes, broken into ten 45-second intervals

Effort: 95%–100% max HR; RPE 9–10

Rest: 1 1/2–2 1/2 minutes

Location: A traffic-free smooth trail, street, or path

Comments: Use the comments in the first workout to guide you. Experiment with sprinkling short, hard sprints throughout a steady workout. Also try 30 seconds or 60 seconds, then keep walking easily between them.

Anaerobic Capacity Workout 3—Unstructured

Measurement: Distance

Length: Four laps of a track, going fast and hard on the long straightaways

Effort: 95%–100% max HR; RPE 9–10

Rest: Walk very slowly and easy on the turns

Location: School track

Comments: This workout is commonly called "straights and turns" because of its structure. If going hard on both straights is too much, then go hard on only one straight each lap, or shorten how far you go hard. Aim for these to feel fast and smooth. Jog out of the sprint at the end if that's more comfortable.

Anaerobic Capacity Workout 4—Structured

Measurement: Distance

Length: 1,500 meters, broken into five 300-meter (3/4-lap) intervals

Effort: 95%–100% max HR; RPE 9–10

Rest: Double the time it takes you to walk the work interval

Location: School track, or trail you've marked in 100-meter increments

Comments: Remember not to get hung up if your track is a 440-yard version, leaving you doing 330-yard intervals for a total of 1,650 yards. The difference is too small to worry about. Do these as fast as you can while maintaining excellent legal form. Never get into a habit of doing workouts so fast that your technique deteriorates.

Anaerobic Capacity Workout 5—Structured

Measurement: Time

Length: 10 minutes, broken into eight 75-second intervals

Effort: 95%–100% max HR; RPE 9–10

Rest: 2 1/2–3 minutes

Location: Any convenient paved trail or path

Comments: This time you'll stick strictly to your watch. Some watches will allow you to program timers that sound at your choice of intervals. If so, set it for 75 seconds, go fast and hard when the first alarm sounds, slow to an easy walk at the second, then repeat, alternating fast and slow with alarms.

Anaerobic Capacity Workout 6—Structured

Measurement: Distance

Length: Approximately 1,200 meters broken into two sets of one each of 300 meters (3/4 of a lap), 200 meters (half a lap), and 100 meters (quarter of a lap)

Effort: 95%–100% max HR; RPE 9–10

Rest: Double or triple the time to walk the work interval

Location: School or community track, or any trail you've marked in 100-meter increments

Comments: Do one complete set of 300-200-100, then repeat the same set. The turnaround between the two sets will be quick, so stay focused. As you progress, these can get longer, such as 400-300-200, adding up to as many sets as you need.

Anaerobic Capacity Workout 7—Structured

Measurement: Distance

Length: 1,100 meters, broken into the following progression—100-200-100-300-100-200-100

Effort: 95%–100% max HR; RPE 9–10

Rest: Double to triple the time for the preceding interval

Table 5.5 Anaerobic Capacity Workouts Summary
Effort: 95–100 percent max HR, RPE 9–10+

Workout	Type	Measurement	Length	Rest	Location
1	Unstructured	Time or landmarks	4 × 90 s	3–4 min	Road or trail
2	Unstructured	Time or landmarks	10 × 45 s	1 1/2–2 1/2 min	Road or trail
3	Unstructured	Distance	8 "straights"	8 × 1 "turn"	Track
4	Structured	Distance	5 × 300 m	Double	Track or marked trail
5	Structured	Time	8 × 75 s	2 1/2–3 min	Road or trail
6	Structured	Distance	(300 m-200 m-100 m-) × 2 sets	Double to triple	Track or marked trail
7	Structured	Distance	100 m-200 m-100 m-300 m-100 m-200 m-100 m	Double to triple	Track

Location: School track

Comments: Imagine the workout as a short pyramid (200-300-200), but you've simply put a 100-meter interval before, between, and after each piece of the pyramid. These can also be lengthened as you get more experience (for example, 200-300-400-300-200, with 100s between each, or even doubling up on the pyramid pieces).

There you have 29 sample workouts covering each of five workout types. With these as templates and the information in the next chapter, you'll be able to start putting together your own training and conditioning program.

CHAPTER 6

TRAINING PROGRAM DESIGN

You're practicing the technique, and you know all about different types of workouts. Those are the pieces to the puzzle. Here's where I offer you instructions about how to combine those pieces to safely build the entire picture of endurance, strength, and speed to meet your training and conditioning goals.

Whether you're interested in racing, successfully walking a local 5- or 10-kilometer weekend event, or priming yourself for a half marathon some months down the road, embarking on a correctly structured training program will help get you there. "Training" isn't only for Olympic hopefuls, you see. Every fitness enthusiast or novice racer is "in training." You will be too.

In this chapter we'll talk about basic training guidelines that apply to every walker, no matter what his or her goal. Note that I won't focus on the marathon distance because it requires an entirely different type of training; rather, we'll only offer a few guidelines to get you started on the really long ones.

We will take a look at training cycles and developmental phases used by the elite athletes to build muscle power and endurance, and how those cycles and phases can apply to your program. With that in mind, we'll offer suggestions about how to analyze individual training goals that give you a way to determine what will work best in your life without overloading your mind and body. Once you're in training, minor strains and pains can happen so we'll cover how to keep them at bay.

BASIC TRAINING GUIDELINES

Just as faster walking doesn't mean going as fast as possible every day, neither does training seriously mean training hard every day, every week, and every month the same old way. Still, training does mean applying a certain overload to your muscles and energy systems—just enough, but not too much—to force them to adapt to the stress with the ability to produce higher levels of strength, speed, and endurance.

Our goal in training, then, is to progressively stress muscles by gradually increasing our distance or speed in workouts at an appropriate pace. When a muscle is stressed and forced to work beyond previous demands, it adapts by making repairs that increase its ability to perform and endure, making you stronger and faster. In endurance training, that means increased blood circulation, increased capillaries in muscle fibers allowing for more efficient oxygen delivery, and stronger connective tissues and muscles. But the body needs a certain amount of rest after long-distance or high-intensity workouts to rebuild and repair itself in these ways so it can reach higher levels, rather than continue to break down.

That's why training programs exist. They follow the guidelines below to help you overload just enough, then rest just enough, without doing too much all at once or the same workout week after week. Remember, though, that every body is different and, if you listen to yours, you'll quickly learn whether you need more or less than the averages we'll establish in this and the next chapter of sample training programs. Now for the guidelines.

ALTERNATE HARD AND EASY WORKOUTS

Hard workouts should not be done on consecutive days. Rather, you need to give yourself at least 48 to 72 hours to recover after more intense workouts before embarking on the next hard one. The older you are, or the less experienced you are, the more recovery time you'll need. That time can be spent doing easy technique-based workouts, easy cross-training, or putting up your feet, depending on your individual needs.

FOLLOW THE 10-TO-20 PERCENT RULE

Research and anecdotal evidence prove that a weekly increase of no more than 10% to 20% in total exercise time or distance works the best. Novice walkers should stick closer to 10%, while veteran walkers or experienced exercisers might jump higher more quickly. For example, if you now walk 20 miles one week, you could safely add from 2 to 4 miles the following week, depending on your experience.

WATCH YOUR TECHNIQUE

Even on easy workouts, warm-ups, or cooldowns, always focus on maintaining good technique. Since most of your time each week is spent in those areas, allowing yourself to walk sloppily will reinforce bad habits that will carry over into the faster workouts aimed at quality training.

HOLD THE INTENSITY 4 TO 6 WEEKS

It's too easy to start racing your own previous workout times each session. Research has shown that it takes the body about 4 to 6 weeks to adapt to a new level of cardiovascular strength. So maintain the same speed for that long before you pump it up a notch. The workouts will start to feel easier and your heart rate will be lower at the same pace.

INCREASE DISTANCE, THEN INTENSITY—NOT BOTH

Avoid changing two variables at once. For example, up the distance and, when that feels comfortable, up the intensity. When that's comfortable, up the distance again. Continue that pattern for safe progression.

REVIEW YOUR PROGRESS MONTHLY

Take a few moments every 4 weeks or so to make sure you're on track. Review your workout logbook to make sure you're following your intended training path, or if you've wavered from it due to enthusiasm or confusion. Use that time to reinforce all the progress you've made. Develop a system to mark workouts that are particularly successful or only moderately so. I use smiley faces, and those faces catch my eye easily when I leaf back through my log.

HAVE A LIFE

Maybe for some this credo is unnecessary. For many of us, however, it can be too easy to get so wrapped up in a goal—especially when it's like a new toy at the holidays—that other things in life and family are neglected. Keep the commitment to your walking training program without losing sight of the rest of your life.

Those are my seven training guidelines. But I'd like to note a few more, put forth by four-time Olympic race walker Carl Schueler during one summer session for race walkers at the Olympic Training Center. Carl drew from nearly two decades of walking, racing, and training to arrive at "Carl's Rules of Race Walking." They are slightly tongue in cheek, but with a strong hint of seriousness. I've added a few explanatory notes to each.

1. **There really aren't any rules**—Rules are made to be broken or, should we say, adapted to our own needs. They are never black and white, but many shades of gray.

2. **People are not the same**—That's why rules are made to be adapted.

3. **Get to know yourself**—So you can adapt the rules to your needs and life.

4. **Rely on your strengths, but also work on your weaknesses**—You might not like, for example, going to the track or doing long workouts, but that's probably because you aren't as good at those workouts. Make yourself work on those weak areas for well-rounded improvement.

5. **Keep an open mind, but use a filter**—Even if the best walker you know has a workout gold standard, or someone you really admire is quoted in a magazine about some nutritional quirk, that doesn't mean you should adopt it. Think those bits through. Do they make sense? Would it really work for you?

6. **There is no one magic pill and probably no magic person**—Not everyone who lectures or conducts workshops can create a magic way to get stronger or faster. Use your filter again.

7. **Flexibility is a big key to technique**—Tight? Stretch to be a better walker. That helps keep your stride relaxed.

8. **The way to straighten your knee is to get off of it (do some cross-training)**—If you're trying to race walk legally with an

extended knee, you might try some cross-training such as swimming or cycling for strengthening or relaxation.

9. **You can't really win a workout (but you can do it perfectly well)**—Forget trying to be speedier every time you train. That might mean you're going too fast or too hard. Sometimes being slower will do you more good.

10. **Don't worry about rules 2 through 9 or especially rule 1.**

ANNUAL TRAINING CYCLES AND PHASES

Serious athletes use a system called "periodization" as the backbone of their training program. The system can be applied to all exercisers who think of themselves as athletes in training, as you should too. In short, periodization means the entire year—or a structured training cycle if shorter than a year—is broken into periods or phases of varying length, with each phase broken into different "cycles." Each phase emphasizes different strength and endurance development goals; each demands a certain length of time to reach that development goal; and each specifies completion at a certain time before your final goal race, event, or season.

The beauty of using the athletic periodization system for all your walking goals is the way it simply and efficiently organizes training. You take the template and slide it into the proper place the proper length of time before your goal event—say you need 20 weeks to prepare, so you take a 20-week period and count back to the appropriate start date. Then you fill in the blanks with your specific workouts that match the underpinnings of each phase and cycle. This system combined with the general physiologic guidelines described earlier acts as your coach or teacher.

For those of us who need mental stimulation, the periodization system also keeps us invigorated and motivated. Your workouts don't just stretch endlessly in front of you, marching identically along, tediously the same week after week. The system requires those who follow it properly to shift in small ways the type, length, and intensity of workouts, as well as total weekly miles, about every 1 or 2 weeks, with major shifts every 1 to 4 months (figure 6.1).

Even if you only want to train to walk faster and stronger without a goal race or event, using periodization can keep you inspired because you'll see logical, incremental progress.

The four components of periodization are:

- **Macrocycle**—As implied by the name, this cycle is the longest. It is one entire training cycle from the start to your event, and could incorporate up to an entire year of training. For participants in some specialty events such as walkathons or marathons, a macrocycle could begin when you start to condition yourself seriously 4 to 6 months prior to an event if you prefer not to structure your training all year.
- **Mesocycle**—A mesocycle is 2 to 6 weeks, with several subsequent mesocycles comprising one developmental phase in the macro training cycle.
- **Microcycle**—This is obviously the shortest cycle, lasting only 1 to 2 weeks. Several microcycles make up one mesocycle.
- **Session**—One workout is a session, the tiniest piece of the periodization puzzle.

Breaking down the training year further into its six developmental phases helps you put into perspective how meso- and microcycles link together to make up the macrocycle. Each phase includes mesocycles of 2 to 6 weeks and microcycles of 1 to 2 weeks.

The length of each phase will depend on your personal goals, horizon of commitment, and fitness background. The ranges are broad, meant to allow you the flexibility to choose not only what best fits your schedule and level of commitment, but also what will best develop your weaknesses and take advantage of your strengths. Note that mileage drops as intensity increases progressively from phase to phase (figure 6.2). Table 6.1 summarizes each of the six phases.

I. GENERAL TRAINING

The goal in this phase is to build aerobic endurance and basic strength, with long workouts being one of the most important pieces of the training during this time. Intensity remains generally low to moderate, with small sprinkles of fartlek. This is one of the best times to do strength training with weights or other resistance and to increase your weekly mileage to nearly its highest level of the year.

Building your mileage is not done continuously, however, but by using microcycles of 1 to 2 weeks, as mentioned above. For example, you might build for two consecutive microcycles, say 2 to 3 weeks total, then take a slight drop of 10% to 20% for a 1-week microcycle. Your progression will look a bit like a jagged stairway as it goes repeatedly up, then down, then back up again as it progresses higher

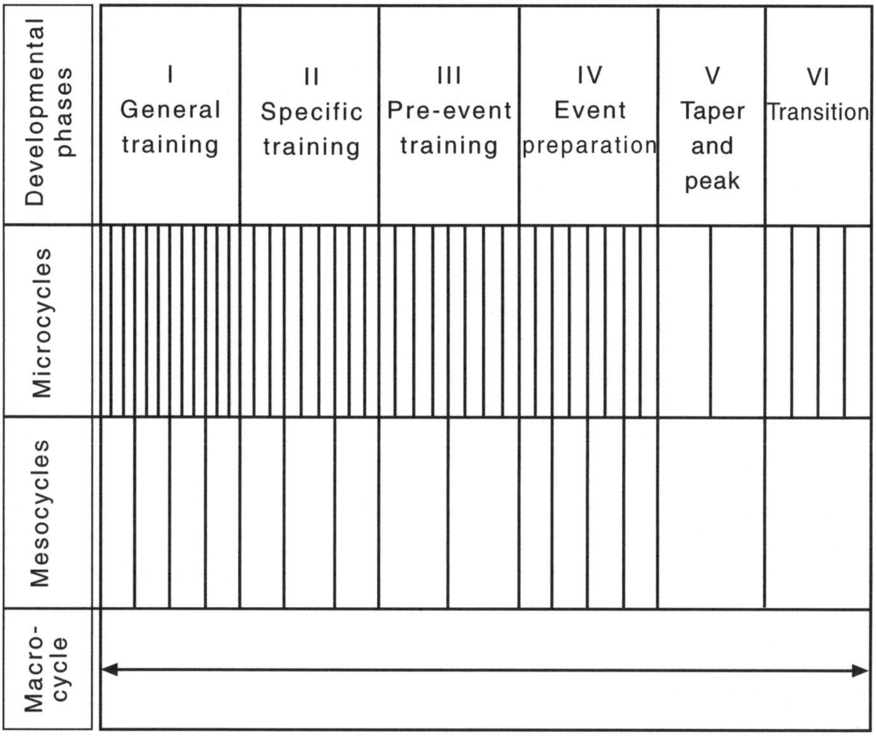

Developmental phases	I General training	II Specific training	III Pre-event training	IV Event preparation	V Taper and peak	VI Transition
Microcycles						
Mesocycles						
Macro-cycle						

Figure 6.1 Breakdown of a macrocycle, showing how phases and cycles fit together.

and higher, allowing you more of a rest in the down week so you'll be able to work harder in the up week. The combination of 2 to 3 "up" weeks and 1 "down" week comprises one mesocycle within this phase.

Length: 4–16 weeks.

II. SPECIFIC TRAINING

The goal is developing your anaerobic threshold, with those workouts taking the front seat in this phase. Mileage doesn't drop too much, since intensity is still moderate. You might begin to throw in occasional aerobic capacity workouts or some speed play bursts during your easy workouts.

Length: 4–16 weeks.

III. PRE-EVENT TRAINING

Threshold development continues, but in this phase the walker begins to add more aerobic capacity workouts to his or her schedule to develop maximal oxygen consumption. Really fast anaerobic capacity workouts are occasionally dropped into the routine. Mileage begins to drop slightly, since intensity is climbing.

Length: 4–12 weeks.

IV. EVENT PREPARATION

Although threshold workouts must not be abandoned in this phase, greater emphasis goes to developing speed and leg turnover without the detrimental effect of excess lactic acid accumulation from too many threshold workouts. The schedule will include more anaerobic capacity workouts, while not abandoning aerobic capacity workouts. Mileage volume drops, especially since a few well-timed practice events step up intensity. Note that this period can lean toward the longer end of the allowed spectrum of weeks if one participates in the community fun races or race walking events that become more frequent in the late spring and through summer. Race walkers often have key regional and national championships starting in May and running into August.

Length: 4–12 weeks.

V. TAPER AND PEAK

This phase is what you do before the event in which you want to perform your best. Tapering involves progressive rest, gradually decreasing mileage, and—for many exercise junkies—pacing the floors and worrying about losing an edge. We'll discuss in greater detail the mechanics of a taper in chapter 8.

Length: 2–3 weeks.

VI. TRANSITION

Perhaps the simplest phase in theory, it asks you to do only a little low-intensity walking, rest a lot, do other activities, and rejuvenate your mind and body for the next macrocycle. This happens at the end of your training or competitive season, such as after a particularly important event or race, or—if you aren't racing or walking events—at the end of the year before you start training again.

Length: 4 weeks.

© Scott Barrow

A few special notes for marathoners, since I am focusing here on shorter distances of a half marathon and less: In the first phase of general training, it is extremely important to establish a strength base. Speed workouts such as aerobic and anaerobic capacity are less important. Your phase for tapering and peaking will be 4 weeks (since you'll be recovering from much lengthier workouts). And your transition phase will be 8 weeks, since 26.2 miles of stress means your body needs more time to replenish and repair before you can begin another macrocycle.

Table 6.1 Developmental Phases of a Training Period

	Goal	Emphasis	Possible length (range in weeks)	Mesocycles	Comments
I. General training	Build aerobic endurance, increase muscle strength, fine-tune technique or resistance training	Long workouts for strength, easy workouts for technique, strength, or resistance training	4–16	1–6	Often called "winter training" because of its timing, caused by relationship to typical track/racing season (May-Aug.).
II. Specific training	Raise threshold, increase stamina to offset lactic acid accumulation, develop event-specific conditioning	Anaerobic threshold workouts, maintain long workouts	4–16	1–6	Drop volume of mileage only slightly from General Training Phase.
III. Pre-event training	Increase speed through $\dot{V}O_2$max development	Aerobic capacity workouts, maintain anaerobic threshold walks	4–12	1–4	Mileage continues to drop sightly (about 10%). Enter some events as a fun training location and to gauge progress.

(continued)

IV. Event preparation test	Increase economy of movement and leg	Anaerobic capacity walks, aerobic turnover alternated, maintain threshold	4–12 capacity workouts	1–4	Further mileage drop (another 5%–10 %), progress in time trials and practice events.
V. Taper and peak	Refresh body and mind, mental preparation for event, achieve peak potential	Short anaerobic capacity workouts, low miles, rest and nutrition	2 (4 if marathon)	1	Do gradually less from beginning to end of taper, but always something.
VI. Transition	Mental and physical recovery, plan for next macrocycle or event	Cross-training, easy walks only for technique maintenance	4 (or longer as needed or desired)	1	Time to rest, think about other activities, and have fun.

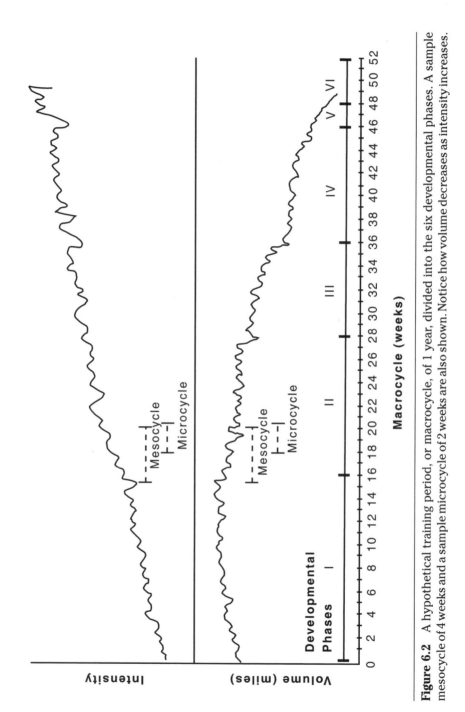

Figure 6.2 A hypothetical training period, or macrocycle, of 1 year, divided into the six developmental phases. A sample mesocycle of 4 weeks and a sample microcycle of 2 weeks are also shown. Notice how volume decreases as intensity increases.

How FAR: Frequency, Amount, Ratio

Piece by piece, I'm laying out the methods of a training program. Earlier you had the workouts, then you learned about training guidelines, next came how to structure the year. The next question isn't as easy to answer—how FAR? Although steeped in science, much of the answer to that question is also an individualistic art:

- **Frequency**—How often should I do a long workout, an anaerobic threshold workout, or any other? How often should I take a day off? How often should I take an easy day?
- **Amount**—How much of each kind of workout should I do? What percentage of my mileage total per micro- or mesocycle should each be? How long should my long workouts be? What's too long? Does it differ depending on my walking goals?
- **Ratio**—What should my work-to-rest ratio be for intervals of different length and intensity?

Take a look at table 6.2. The guidelines there will answer those questions. Notice as interval, or noncontinuous, workouts become more intense, the length of rest you may take between them gets longer. If you are walking 6 days a week, you will be able each week to fit in nearly every kind of workout you want during a phase. In addition, you might be able to calculate the maximum safe percentage of your mileage totals for each workout type, as specified on the table, using your weekly mileage. However, if you are only walking three or four times a week, or are older or less experienced, allow yourself to see the larger picture of total mesocycle mileage divided by its microcycles to calculate safe maximums for each workout type; it could cause injury to try to squeeze in multiple hard workouts each week at lower total mileage. In this case, feel free to break out of the constraints of a 7-day week, expanding your microcycle to 10 or 14 days so you not only have time to fit in the workouts you want, but also enough rest between them.

Remember that these are only guidelines, not commandments etched in stone. View the suggested volume as an upper limit. Take the ratio of work to rest as a recommendation. Some days you might need a little more. Better to complete the workout successfully by taking 15 or 30 seconds more rest, than be so tired that you can't move at the end.

Table 6.2   How FAR: Frequency, Amount, Ratio

	Conditioning goal	Frequency	Amount	Ratio (work:rest)	Example
Easy	Technique fine-tuning, recovery, strength building	As needed	As needed	n/a	Continuous 30–60 min
Long	Aerobic conditioning, soft tissue strengthening, technique and endurance	One every 7–10 days (one every microcycle)	No more than 25%–30% of mesocycle mileage, divided between microcycles	n/a	Continuous 60–120 min, or 1/2 AM and 1/2 PM (marathoners will build to 4–6 h)
Anaerobic threshold	Raise threshold at which body can efficiently produce aerobic energy (i.e., increase speed when aerobic)	1–2 every week or microcycle (maximum every 48–72 h)	Up to 60 min total per week or microcycle, or up to 20%–25% of total mesocycle mileage in 2–3 sessions	20%–30 % rest, e.g., 5 min work earns 60–90 s rest, or 5:1–5:1.5	5–20 min intervals, or one of 15–40 min continuous effort

(continued)

Aerobic capacity	Improve and quicken efficient use of oxygen by body	0–2 every week or microcycle (maximum every 48–72 h)	Up to 10% of total mesocycle mileage in 1–2 sessions, divided between microcycles	Rest equal to work, e.g., 1:1	3–9 min intervals
Anaerobic capacity	Improve speed and biomechanical efficiency	0–2 per week (maximum every 48–72 h). *During taper, you might do more, but fewer miles per session.	< or = 5% of total mesocycle mileage in 1–2 sessions (approximately up to 1–2 mi per session)	Full rest (double or triple), e.g., 1:2–1:3	Intervals of 30 s to 2 min

REST AND OVERTRAINING

Vital to any training program is the rest planned into it. Without rest, burnout and overtraining could be around the corner for any level of exerciser.

REST

Perhaps you've noticed how well-planned the amount of rest is as a component of a sane training program. Rest is perhaps the most important part of a program and sometimes one of the most neglected. Take a look at Yakovlev's model of supercompensation (figure 6.3). The theory behind the three-decade old model can be applied to a single session, a microcycle, mesocycle, or macrocycle. The "rest" pictured by the curves below the line represents the rest between intervals, the easy and off days in a microcycle, the "down" week in a mesocycle, or the transition and recovery period in a macrocycle.

Whichever you use as a comparison, the message is clear: Do too much and you won't achieve your goal or reach your potential. You'll

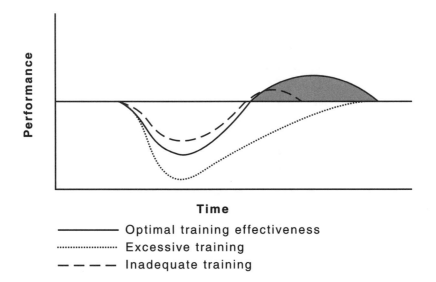

Figure 6.3   The Yakovlev model of supercompensation illustrates how the right amount of training can produce the desired effect, while too much or too little won't.
Adapted from Martin and Coe 1991.

also risk burnout and physiologic/emotional overtraining. On the other hand, do too little and you still won't achieve what you want because you won't have stressed your body enough to achieve gains. Note, though, that any good training program does cause some overload to the muscles and cardiovascular system. Knowing when you've hit the maximum overload you can tolerate without exploding is the artful part behind the science of training.

OVERTRAINING

You don't have to be an Olympian knocking off more than a hundred miles a week to fall prey to this beast. What's the right amount of training and rest for one person might be too much or too little for you; what's the right speed for easy or long workouts for another might be too intense for you; what's the right number of threshold or aerobic capacity workouts per macrocycle for yet another walker might be too many for you.

In addition, what's going on in the rest of your life can affect what is too much or just enough. If you're trying to hold down a full-time job, nurture a relationship, or go to night school and raise a child, less will feel like much more than if you are just going to school and working out or are retired. "You only have so much motivation, intensity, and energy to give to the world," says Marjorie Snyder, PhD, sport psychologist, and associate executive director of the Women's Sports Foundation. "If your work life and your personal life are going at the same pace, and you step up your training, something has to go."

"Less is more," Bruce Ogilvie, PhD, one of the founding fathers of sport psychology, also told me once. With his probing questions one year, I had come to realize I was direly overtrained. But for several previous months of diminishing returns in training, I kept looking elsewhere for reasons: lack of sleep, electrolyte imbalance, iron deficiencies, maybe a heart problem? Nothing was confirmed, but I felt irritable and depressed. Workouts that should have been easy were difficult. I had a deep, aching muscle soreness that didn't go away even after easy workouts. I was on the edge emotionally, snapping at friends, and sleeping poorly.

Ogilvie, after looking at a simple questionnaire I'd filled out at a track meet as part of a research project he was conducting, said to me: "You try too hard, and you're so damn impatient. Don't let the pressure get to you. . . . Are you sure you aren't overtrained?"

I was, I finally admitted to myself a few days later. And I know all too well how difficult it is to dig back out of the hole because it looks so dark and bleak when you're down there.

Interestingly, overtraining begins to manifest itself (see table 6.3) first with emotional and behavioral changes, such as a short temper,

Table 6.3 Symptoms of Overtraining

• **Sleep** — Do you take longer to fall asleep, awake during the night more frequently, and sleep less restfully?

• **Appetite** — Are you less hungry, eating less, or sometimes so tired you don't feel like eating?

• **Thirst** — Are you thirstier or drinking more in the evening?

• **Muscle soreness** — Do you ache more than usual, even after easy workouts or when you're not working out?

• **Perceived exertion** — Do workouts feel harder than they used to, even at the same intensity or speed as before?

• **Mood** — Do you feel blue, tense, anxious, depressed, argument-prone, impatient, or more easily upset than usual?

• **Training** — Are you unable to complete previously manageable training loads or paces, or has your performance plateaued or deteriorated despite short rests or tapers?

• **Heart rate** — Is your resting pulse 5–10 beats per minute higher than usual, and does your workout heart rate jump higher than usual, perhaps at slower paces?

high anxiety, restless sleep, and emotional imbalances. Once you've reached the physiologically telling symptoms of higher resting heart rates and a lower anaerobic threshold, you've gone past the point of no return. But note that a higher resting pulse isn't always a sure sign of doing too much. In some people, the resting pulse doesn't go up and may even go down.

"By the time we're able to pick up solid physiological indicators, the person is definitely overtrained," says Dr. Rudy Dressendorfer, exercise physiology professor. He's been studying overtraining since 1979, and is still searching for a black-and-white clue to help exercisers and coaches know when enough is enough. Somewhat dejectedly, he admits, "The psychologists can beat us there every time in detecting overtraining."

So, keep tabs on your emotions and behavior. They are your early warning system. Nevertheless, don't neglect checking physiological clues, such as your daily resting and workout pulse. To take a proper resting heart rate, count your pulse when you wake up in the morning, before you've gotten out of bed or moved much, or are even fully awake—a wireless heart rate monitor is the most accurate method. Once you establish your normal resting pulse, you'll be able to note days when it's higher by about 5 to 10 beats per minute as a signal that you need some rest, or are stressed, getting sick, or overtrained.

Also, note your ambient heart rate at certain times each day. For example, I note my pre-workout heart rate each morning after being up an hour or so, and compare the numbers day to day to make sure they don't jump. I've found higher readings often signal an impending illness or the lack of sleep.

Remember, preventing overtraining is easier than recovering from it. Know the symptoms, but also realize that everyone experiences different ones first or at different intensities. The tips in table 6.4 will help you recognize and prevent overtraining.

Table 6.4   Preventing Overtraining

- **Keep a workout log.**
  1. **Rate your feelings** — Be concrete, using a scale such as 1–5, so you can better compare workouts. Consistently hitting a low of 1s and 2s (mood) or a high of 4s and 5s (fatigue) may be an early warning of overtraining.
  2. **Note your enjoyment** — Rate how much fun you had: trouble might not be far off when the fun stops.
  3. **Record your sleep** — Write down the hours as well as the restfulness and quality.
- **Be flexible** — If your body says it's tired, change your course or workout or add another rest day.
- **Take care of your mind** — Do something nice for yourself unrelated to athletics, such as a trip to a museum, a peaceful evening with a distracting novel, or a pampering massage.
- **Determine your personal indicators** — Tune into what might mean you are edging toward trouble, such as impatience or an inability to focus on work.

STAYING INJURY FREE

Keeping yourself mentally and physiologically sound with sane workouts and enough well-scheduled rest is one part of a good training program. Maintaining a physically sound body also plays an important role in an uninterrupted training program.

Walking might be virtually injury free because of its low impact per foot strike (about 1 to 1 1/2 times your body weight compared to running's 3 to 4 times), but that doesn't mean you'll never get a tweak, twinge, strain, or sprain. For example, you might be genetically predisposed to injury because of bone structure or joint alignment, such as bow legs or a spinal curve.

Genetic factors are beyond your control. Within your control, however, are the best injury-reduction factors, including proper warm-ups and cooldowns, stretching, strengthening, and cross-training workouts.

Watch most walkers or runners at a trail or track someday. You'll find many never stretch before or after, and I'd hedge a bet that they don't strengthen much either. Often, warm-ups and cooldowns are only the short walk from car to trail, and from trail back to the car. My guess is, either these people don't think attention to warming up and cooling down is necessary because they're "only" walking, or they let that part of the program slide because of lack of time. Remember, training to walk for performance and higher conditioning will demand more from your muscles than sidling along at a flower-smelling pace.

A brief overview here of ways to help you stay injury free can allow you to better plan your training program. If you want more information, appendix A offers additional resources that focus in greater detail on how to stretch and strengthen. In addition my book, *Fitness Walking* (Human Kinetics, 1995), has chapters on warming up and cooling down with walking-specific stretches, as well as specific recommendations for cross-training. Take those few extra minutes each day or several times a week to warm up, stretch, cool down, strengthen, and cross train before an injury sidelines you.

WARM-UP

Warming up before a workout prepares not only your body, but also your mind, for the walk ahead. Physiologically, spending a few minutes at the beginning of each walk moving a little slower, swinging your arms, shaking your legs, and stopping to stretch allows your body temperature to rise gradually, softens your muscles so they're more pliable and ready to respond to the demands of your workout, releases lubricating fluid in your joints so your bones move more easily, and warms up your heart muscle and cardiovascular system.

Psychologically, the time you spend allows your mind to think through what you're going to ask your body to perform and either wake up (for morning workouts) or transition smoothly from work and daily business (for midday or evening workouts).

The structure and length of a warm-up varies from person to person and between different types of workouts. For easy and long workouts, your warm-up can be the first few minutes of your walk; all you do is walk more slowly at the beginning and stop to loosen up your muscles after a few minutes before continuing the rest of the day's mileage. For moderate to hard workouts, such as anaerobic threshold or aerobic capacity walks, you'll want to spend 20 to 30 minutes gradually increasing your speed and turnover and stopping to stretch once or twice. Think of your warm-up in stages:

- **Stage I**—Very easy to easy walking, 4 to 12 minutes. Heart rate remains below 60% of maximum. After this stage, do your first stretch—an initial loosening of muscles, including arm circles, leg swings from the hip, and shoulder rolls.

- **Stage II**—Moderate walking, 5 to 10 minutes. Heart rate climbs gradually to about 70% to 75% of maximum. After this stage, do your second stretch—more concentrated stretching, focusing on any individual problem areas.

- **Stage III**—Fast walking, 2 to 5 minutes of alternating short bursts of speed with very easy recovery. Heart rate climbs slightly higher (75% to 85%), but only for 30 to 60 seconds at a time.

For moderate workouts, such as some threshold walks, you might be able to stop after stage II. The speedy pickups just before you start are especially important to kick your legs into faster gear for aerobic and anaerobic capacity interval workouts. But you must be your own coach and learn how much works for you and whether you need more time to mentally immerse yourself in the work ahead. Discovering how to do the best warm-up for you also takes practice.

COOLDOWN

Think of the cooldown as the warm-up in reverse. You walk gradually slower for 6 to 12 minutes, then stop to stretch. Usually, the more intense the workout, the longer you'll need to cool down and allow your heart and muscles to make a smooth transition back to their resting state. During the cooldown, the amount and direction of blood flow is readjusted from muscles back to vital organs and skin. Your heart rate adjusts slowly downward. Body temperature decreases gradually.

If you stop suddenly, enough blood might not get pumped to your head, causing light-headedness or dizziness. Sometimes you might experience irregular heartbeats as the body readjusts—a dangerous phenomenon if you have heart problems.

Stretching after your heart rate has returned to resting allows your muscles, after forcefully contracting during your workout, to return to an elongated state and might increase flexibility. Post-workout muscle soreness might also be avoided if you cool down and stretch diligently.

STRETCHING

As a walker, you need to stretch as much and as often as any other exercisers, especially if you're pushing your body to its personal limit. To perform a proper stretch, hold each position 15 to 30 seconds just to the point of tension without bouncing. Bouncing can not only strain muscles, but also tighten muscles due to a protective response in the fibers. Breathe deeply into each stretch, allowing yourself to relax farther into the stretch with each exhalation.

Pay close attention to areas where you experience particular tightness. For example, those who have trouble straightening their knees might want to spend extra time working on their calves and backs of the legs. Those who have problems slumping forward could spend more time stretching open their chest and shoulders. Someone who has a swayback will make sure his or her hip flexors and low back are as loose as possible.

All walkers should pay attention to the muscles responsible for propelling, braking, and stabilizing their movements. Many muscles serve several functions, but below is a summary list by major function.

- **Propulsive muscles:** Feet, shins, ankles, calves, gluteals, hip flexors, back, and shoulders.
- **Braking muscles:** Feet, shins, hamstrings.
- **Stabilizing muscles:** Iliotibial band (side of your leg), gluteals, quadriceps.

The more stretching the better, especially after your workout when your muscles are soft and warm. Three walker-specific stretches not to be missed are the iliotibial band, the hamstring, and the calf.

ILIOTIBIAL BAND

The iliotibial band (ITB) is a tendinous band that runs from the side of your hip to just below your knee. It works overtime to balance you with every step and may get an extra stretch from the hip flexion, extension, and rotation of walking. To stretch it properly, you need to keep the knee joint extended, since the lower end attaches below the knee.

Stand about an arm's length from a wall, placing the palm of the hand against the wall. Cross the outside leg to the front and over the inside leg. Maintaining the torso's vertical position parallel to the wall, move the torso toward the wall. The front knee bends, while the rear leg remains straight. You will be stretching the ITB of the rear leg. Allow your supporting elbow to bend as much as needed to keep your torso vertical as you sink toward the wall. Be sure to keep the outside hip dropped, rather than letting it hike upward. Repeat on the other side.

HAMSTRING

The hamstring is a group of three muscles—semimembranosus, semitendinosus, and biceps femoris—in the rear of the leg that runs from the lower pelvis to the back of the knee. This muscle group works hard in a stretched position to brake the stride to the front, and helps propel you strongly forward from the rear leg.

Sit on a bench. Place your right leg, knee extended, on the bench. Turn your torso so your hips and chest face the extended leg. Now sit up tall from your low back. You might already feel a stretch in the back of your upper leg. If you need an additional stretch, maintain the tall position with chest upright and neck aligned with the spine. Reach your sternum slightly toward your toes. You should avoid rounding your low back, dropping your chin to your chest, or your forehead toward your knee. Repeat on the other side.

CALF

The calf is the thick knot in the rear of your lower leg that flattens out toward the Achilles and consists of two muscles, the gastrocnemius and the soleus. It must contract repeatedly to propel you forward.

Stand on the edge of a curb with your toes on the surface and your heels hanging off it. To stretch the gastrocnemius, lower one heel toward the ground slowly to the point of tension and hold. Be careful not to sink too far, too quickly. Repeat on the other side. To stretch the soleus, lower the heel toward the ground and bend the knee. Hold and repeat.

Refer to the previous summary of major propulsive, stabilizing, and braking muscles to note which areas of your body you should stretch as a part of your program. You can use these names to look up additional stretches that might be appropriate for you in specialty books in appendix A.

STRENGTHENING

Even the most flexible muscle won't be able to respond properly if it isn't strong enough, and a weak muscle will be more prone to injury. When you strengthen muscles, it's important to maintain balance by working opposing muscle groups. For example, if you strengthen the quadriceps, don't miss the hamstrings; if you work the shins, be sure to exercise your calves.

A well-rounded program is best, allowing you to hit all parts of your body. Free weights and machines in health clubs offer ideal surroundings, but you can accomplish the same thing in your living room with push-ups, pull-ups, and sit-ups, as well as with exercises using resistance from large rubberized exercise bands.

Again, you'll want to pay extra attention to your susceptible areas. Hamstring pains might indicate the need for strengthening work; trouble keeping your chest open and shoulders back could mean more back strengthening is needed; an inability to maintain a good heel strike and roll-through might be a sign of weak shins.

Pay attention to the same muscles previously listed under the stretching section. A health club trainer or good book on strengthening from appendix A will help get you started. Meanwhile, work on two specific muscles, the shin and the hamstring, can help your training program.

SHIN

This muscle is in the front of the lower leg and consists of the tibialis anterior and peroneal group. The shins get a particular beating in walking because of the requirement to strongly lift the toes and roll through the foot. When you first start, you might feel some burning or extra fatigue in the front or side of the lower leg. Use ice before and after your walk, stretch, and strengthen the shins, and soon you'll walk pain free.

Attach an exercise band to the leg of a chair. Sit on the ground facing the band with your legs extended, hooking the toes of one foot through the band. Keep the band taut while you flex your foot to bring the toes as far toward your torso as possible, then slowly point your foot straight ahead, also keeping the band taut. Work up to 15 to 20 repetitions per foot. Also do several repetitions in which you alternate flexing your foot with pointing your toes to the side, as if drawing a half moon. Repeat on the other side.

HAMSTRING

Lie on your stomach with your feet facing the exercise band hooked to the leg of the chair. Hook the band around your ankle. Keeping your hip bones and abdominals on the ground and your back relaxed, bring your heel toward your gluteals. The band will provide resistance and force your hamstrings to work. Work up to 10 to 12 repetitions with each leg.

CROSS-TRAINING

No matter how healthy and injury free walking is, you'll need to give your body a break from the continual, repeated stresses of the identical linear motion. Your mind could also use an occasional break from the same routine. If you are serious about racing, cross-training will have to be planned carefully into your training program so it doesn't leave you sore or tired for your important walking workouts. If you're walking for performance and personal challenges, cross-training activities could occasionally substitute for walking workouts. For example, an intense hike might take the place of a moderate tempo workout, while a leisurely bike ride could replace an easy workout. Anyone can add a different activity once a week or so, depending on his or her walking program.

Since walkers demand so much power in linear movement from their gluteals, hamstrings, and calves, ideal cross-training activities might include activities that use different muscles or the same ones in different patterns, depending on your cross-training goal. For example, cycling uses more quadriceps, while tennis allows you to move laterally and backward, and swimming uses more upper body.

Deep-water running workouts can also complement your training program, getting you off your feet while still allowing you to get an intense workout. In these, you wear a flotation vest. This allows you to concentrate on simulating a running movement with knees and arms pumping without having to worry about staying afloat. Know that if you use a heart rate monitor, your heart rate will range from 10% to 20% lower in water workouts, partly because the water pressure surrounding your body helps pump the blood. Cross-check your intensity by listening to your perceived exertion.

Deep-water workouts can be an addictive and refreshing change in your training program. Structure interval workouts based on time to best replicate walking workouts. For example, if you do quarter-mile repeats on the road or track in 2 1/2 minutes with equal rest of 2 1/2 minutes then paddle hard for 2 1/2 minutes and rest 2 1/2 minutes. Water workouts can also keep you fit while recovering from ankle sprains or other lower-body strains.

CHAPTER 7

SAMPLE TRAINING PROGRAMS

Now for the fun part. Here's where you get to take the various types of workouts, the samples of those workout types, and the principles of training programs, and put it all together. The series of samples here will help you see how these concepts fit together so you'll be able to design your own training and conditioning program.

These sample training programs are conceived to show you how you can succeed at your goal event or race, or even at a hard workout with friends, without resorting to slogging along with head drooping, arms down, and tail dragging. If these concepts and samples are followed correctly as you begin to outline your own workouts and training program, you should be able to complete your goal at a reasonable, successful pace.

Let's take a moment to see where you can begin, depending on how much you've been walking in the past. Take a look back at chapter 2 where you thought about your short- and long-term goals and truthfully assessed your fitness level, technique, and experience. Now, take a moment to complete this short quiz, circling the answer that best suits your desires:

Do you want to:

1. a. devote unlimited time and energy?
   b. give about an hour 5 to 6 days a week?
   c. invest about 45 minutes, 4 to 5 times a week?

2. a. embark on a long-term training and racing program with a possible goal of higher level racing?
   b. undertake one specific distance event or half marathon at a strong pace?
   c. complete a local 5K or 10K event?

3. a. plan mostly structured workouts based on distance?
   b. plan a mix of structured and unstructured workouts?
   c. plan only unstructured workouts based on time?

4. a. look ahead a year or more?
   b. look ahead 6 to 8 months?
   c. look ahead 4 to 5 months?

5. What is your walking experience?
   a. 45 to 60 minutes, 5 to 7 times a week, for 6 to 10 months.
   b. 30 to 45 minutes, 4 to 5 times a week, for 4 to 6 months.
   c. 25 to 35 minutes, 3 to 4 times a week, for 2 to 3 months.

If you answered mostly *a,* you're ready to get serious and can go straight to Race Training programs. They will prep you for racing and training all year, enabling you to maintain a fast pace in 10- and 20-kilometer events up to a half marathon, with possible competition at higher levels.

If you answered mostly *b,* Sport Training programs will help you successfully complete a steady 10-kilometer fun event, or a long-distance walk such as a fund-raising walkathon or half marathon, especially if you have some base fitness conditioning.

If you answered mostly *c,* refer to the Novice Training programs. Pick a local short-distance event in 4 to 5 months (a 5K preferably, or perhaps 10K, if you're willing to commit a little more time each week) and start training now to be able to accomplish your goal.

In the following pages are three sets of program samples—one each for Novice Training (for those with some experience, but who are new to this level of training or speed), Sport Training (for the more experienced, but those with shorter-term or less-competitive goals), and Race Training (for those who truly want to race and to commit to more in-depth training for the long term).

For each program, you will find:

1. one broad overview of a training cycle (a macrocycle) that shows you each development phase, the number of weeks in a sample phase, and offers comments about workout development within the phase appropriate to the sample walker's experience level.

2. four sample weeks—one for each of the first four phases of the macrocycle—that show how a week's workouts might be put together. There, you'll also find the approximate percentage of total miles in a mesocycle allotted to that workout, and any special notes about the week or workout alternatives to consider. Note that when calculating workout mileage based on mesocycle totals, you should attempt to divide those miles between microcycles.

Note that Development Phase V (Taper and Peak), has not been included here, since I will discuss it in detail in the next chapter about racing. You see, a taper might not be necessary for some walkers who just want to work out hard to attain excellent conditioning and might not want to truly peak to race. And a taper and peak not only isn't necessary, but also isn't advised for every event.

In addition, the details of a Transition Phase (VI) haven't been included in these sample weeks, since a transition means simply to walk very little and very easily, rest a lot, and do other activities of personal choice, as explained in the previous chapter. That could mean cycling, aerobic dance, rock climbing, hiking, or basketball. No one else but you can prescribe what other activities you should do in your transition and recovery from structured walking workouts. In fact, a formal transition phase might not be needed at all if you only do one macrocycle a year and it is 10 months long or less. For example, if you train for 6 months, do a half marathon, and are done until the next year, you have 6 months to "transition." Whereas, if you are building a racing plan for the next 4 years, you'll need to plan 4 weeks off when it fits best with your program, perhaps in the late summer or early fall.

Remember that these samples can't be all things to all people of all levels of all goals. They are strictly an average slice of a typical macrocycle and how its associated developmental phases would be built for average walkers of each of the three types we've addressed. Avoid seeing them as black-and-white pictures, but look instead for the shades of gray. Notice how these could be altered to best fit your needs and schedule. For example, you could increase or decrease percentages of a workout type, slide the rest day to a different spot, lengthen or shorten the developmental phase, or alternate certain types of workouts within one phase. (There will be notes about such things in the comment sections.) The combinations are endless. Use your imagination to create your personal program. Table 7.1 details the abbreviations used in the weekly samples.

Table 7.1   Workout Name Abbreviations

Workout type	Abbreviation
Easy	EZ
Long	Long
Anaerobic threshold/interval	AT/interval
Anaerobic threshold/continuous	AT/ continuous
Aerobic capacity	AC
Anaerobic capacity	AnC

NOVICE TRAINING PROGRAM

Assumptions: You have limited time to train, a short-term focus or goal event, and minimal walking experience.

Possible goals: Completion of a 5-kilometer or 10-kilometer event or charity walk. Build overall fitness, strength, and speed for personal satisfaction.

Pre-program mileage: Minimum of 10–15 miles weekly.

Program mileage: Starting at 12–16 miles, progressing to 16–24 miles weekly.

Comments: After completing Novice Training if you are at the lower end of the starting mileage, you might need a lengthier

Sample Macrocycle—Novice Training Program

Development phase	Weeks in phase	Week ranges	Comments
I. General training	6	1–6	Increase mileage 10% per week, up to 50% overall by end of phase. Start AT at 10% per session and increase to 15% of mesocycle mileage, with miles divided between microcycles. Mix in AT/continuous workouts.
II. Specific training	4	7–10	Hold mileage steady first 2 weeks. After 3rd week, decrease mileage 5% per week through end of Phase IV (if you have a goal event).
III. Pre-event training	4	11–14	Complete a long workout the 1st and 3rd weeks. Find a practice event or a weekend run to walk in the 2nd week.
IV. Event preparation	4	15–18	Find a practice event in the 3rd week. Eliminate long walks the last 2 weeks (if you have a goal event).
V. Taper and peak	2	19–20	Mileage drops by 50% overall into week of event if one is scheduled.
VI. Transition	4	21–24	As needed.

Sample Weeks—Novice Training Program

Phase I

Day 1 Monday	Day 2 Tuesday	Day 3 Wednesday	Day 4 Thursday	Day 5 Friday	Day 6 Saturday	Day 7 Sunday
Rest	AT/continuous 10%	Rest	AT/interval 10%	Rest	EZ	Long 25%

Comments: 1. Make sure you have at least 1–2 days rest after a long workout.
2. AT totals may start at 20% and progress to 25%–30% of total mesocycle mileage.

Phase II

Day 1 Monday	Day 2 Tuesday	Day 3 Wednesday	Day 4 Thursday	Day 5 Friday	Day 6 Saturday	Day 7 Sunday
Rest	AT/interval 15%	EZ	AT/interval 15%	Rest	EZ	Long 30%

Comments: 1. Put more emphasis on AT workouts.
2. Consider adding some speed play to one EZ workout each week or microcycle.

Phase III

Day 1 Monday	Day 2 Tuesday	Day 3 Wednesday	Day 4 Thursday	Day 5 Friday	Day 6 Saturday	Day 7 Sunday
EZ	AT/interval 20%	Rest	AC 5%	Rest	EZ	Long 20%

Comments: 1. Keep your first few AC workouts lower in total mileage.
2. Alternate weeks with longer workouts.

Phase IV

Day 1 Monday	Day 2 Tuesday	Day 3 Wednesday	Day 4 Thursday	Day 5 Friday	Day 6 Saturday	Day 7 Sunday
Rest	AnC 3%	EZ	AT/interval 10%	Rest	EZ	AT/interval 15%

Comments: 1. You might not do a long workout every week in Phase IV.

program to build enough fitness to complete a goal event. Whatever length your program, if you plan to walk an event, try to choose it when you begin the program. Use the event as a motivating tool to keep you working throughout the training program. Because of short phases, each phase is one meso-cycle.

SPORT TRAINING PROGRAM

Assumptions: You have at least several months of experience and are willing to devote more time, although perhaps not an entire year.

Possible goals: Strong finish of a 10-kilometer event or other distance event up to a half marathon, although a longer event goal will be slower.

Pre-program mileage: Minimum of 14–20 miles weekly.

Program mileage: Starting at 15–22 miles weekly, progressing to 23–35 miles weekly.

Comments: Avoid starting your mileage too high and progressing too quickly. Give your body time to adapt to the increased stresses.

RACE TRAINING PROGRAM

Assumptions: You are willing to invest whatever time is needed to accomplish your goals, with possible intentions of high-level racing. You are likely looking ahead one or more years.

Possible goals: Top racing effort up to half marathon.

Pre-program mileage: Minimum of 20–30 miles weekly.

Program mileage: Starting at 20–30 miles weekly, progressing to 30–45 miles weekly.

Comments: Even if you are not serious about racing, you could follow this plan to achieve gains in strength and speed for personal satisfaction.

Sample Macrocycle—Sport Training Program

Development phase	Weeks in phase	Week ranges	Comments
I. General training	8	1–8	Increase mileage by 50% over the 8-week phase. AT workouts increase from 10% to 15% per session, with total miles divided between microcycles. Complete two 4-week mesocycles.
II. Specific training	6	9–14	Hold mileage steady over first 3 weeks. Over next 15 weeks, decrease miles 3% per week. Alternate AC with AT every 2nd or 3rd week of total mesocycle mileage.
III. Pre-event training	6	15–20	Schedule two practice events or time trials. Start AnC workouts, possibly alternating 2 weeks of AC with 1 week of AnC.
IV. Event preparation	6	21–26	Schedule two practice events and a time trial at two-thirds of distance of goal event. Alternate AnC and AC. No long walk last 2 weeks before event.
V. Taper and peak	2	27–28	Mileage drops 50% into event week.
VI. Transition	2	29–30	As needed.

Sample Weeks—Sport Training Program

Phase I

	Day 1 Monday	Day 2 Tuesday	Day 3 Wednesday	Day 4 Thursday	Day 5 Friday	Day 6 Saturday	Day 7 Sunday
	Rest	AT/interval 10%	EZ	Rest	AT/continuous 10%–15%	EZ	Long 25%

Comments: 1. Start with alternating AT/intervals and AT/continuous workouts.

2. Consider adding short speed play of 30 seconds to an occasional easy workout.

Phase II

	Day 1 Monday	Day 2 Tuesday	Day 3 Wednesday	Day 4 Thursday	Day 5 Friday	Day 6 Saturday	Day 7 Sunday
	EZ	AT/interval 15%	EZ	AT/interval 10%	Rest	EZ	Long 30%

Comments: 1. Reach and hold 25% of mesocycle mileage as AT workouts.

2. Alternate an AT workout with an AC workout every 2nd or 3rd week.

Phase III

	Day 1 Monday	Day 2 Tuesday	Day 3 Wednesday	Day 4 Thursday	Day 5 Friday	Day 6 Saturday	Day 7 Sunday
	AT/interval 10%	EZ	AT/interval 10%	Rest	AC 5%–8%	EZ	Long 25%

Comments: 1. Avoid overdoing speedy AC workouts when introducing them weekly.

2. If you need extra rest, eliminate one AT workout per week per microcycle.

Phase IV

	Day 1 Monday	Day 2 Tuesday	Day 3 Wednesday	Day 4 Thursday	Day 5 Friday	Day 6 Saturday	Day 7 Sunday
	EZ	AT/interval 20%	EZ	AnC 5%	Rest	EZ	Practice event

Comments: 1. Avoid long walks in the 2 weeks before your event; they will overtire you.

Sample Macrocycle—Race Training Program

Development phase	Weeks in phase	Week ranges	Comments
I. General training	14	1–14	Increase miles 50% to 70% above starting mileage during Phase 1. Gradually increase AT workouts from 10% to 25% of mesocycle total mileage, with total miles divided between microcycles.
II. Specific training	12	15–26	Hold mileage steady first 4 weeks. Over next 8 weeks, drop mileage 15% to 20% overall. AT workouts hold 20–25% of mileage. Do an AC workout every 3rd week instead of an additional AT workout.
III. Pre-event training	9	27–35	Mileage drops 10% in Phase III with the addition of AC's higher intensity. Schedule two practice races or time trials. Introduce AnC training in week prior to practice event. AC reaches 7% maximum mileage.
IV. Event preparation	10	36–45	Schedule two to three practice races or time trials. Over first 6 weeks, mileage fluctuates dropping as much as 20% before races or time trials but returning to starting level afterward. Over last 4 weeks, mileage drops 8% from mileage at beginning of phase.
V. Taper and peak	3	46–48	Mileage drops 50% into race week.
VI. Transition	4	49–52	Only easy walking combined with other activities.

Sample Weeks—Race Training Program

Phase I

Day 1 Monday	Day 2 Tuesday	Day 3 Wednesday	Day 4 Thursday	Day 5 Friday	Day 6 Saturday	Day 7 Sunday
EZ	AT/interval 10%	EZ	AT/continuous 10%	Rest	EZ with fartlek	Long 30%

Comments: 1. Add speed play (fartlek) once a week on an easy workout day.

2. Maintain strong and steady long workouts.

Phase II

Day 1 Monday	Day 2 Tuesday	Day 3 Wednesday	Day 4 Thursday	Day 5 Friday	Day 6 Saturday	Day 7 Sunday
AT/interval 10%	EZ	AT/continuous 7%	Rest	EZ	AT/interval 5%	Long 20%–25%

Comments: 1. Every 3rd week, do an AC workout instead of one of the AT/interval workouts.

2. Emphasize strong AT workouts.

(continued)

Sample Weeks—Race Training Program (continued)

Phase III

Day 1 Monday	Day 2 Tuesday	Day 3 Wednesday	Day 4 Thursday	Day 5 Friday	Day 6 Saturday	Day 7 Sunday
EZ	AT/interval 15%	EZ	Rest	AC 7%	EZ	Long 25%

Comments: 1. Build interesting AC ladders and pyramids to keep you motivated.

Phase IV

Day 1 Monday	Day 2 Tuesday	Day 3 Wednesday	Day 4 Thursday	Day 5 Friday	Day 6 Saturday	Day 7 Sunday
EZ	AT/interval 15%	EZ	Rest	AnC 5%	EZ	Long 20%

Comments: 1. Alternate AC (7%–8%) with AnC (5%) every other week.

2. Avoid a long workout during the 2 weeks before your race.

TIPS ON MARATHON CONDITIONING

One additional note for those interested in marathon walking, since our samples don't directly address such long-distance endeavors: If you have some base conditioning, you should be able to choose an event to be held in 4 to 6 months, train well, and complete it successfully, albeit not necessarily fast. Success will require building your weekly long walk to 18 or 20 miles. Once you reach 14 or 16 miles on your long walk, alternate a longer walk one week with a slightly shorter one the next. For example, your long walk progression might appear, in miles, something like this: 6-8-10-12-14-16-12-18-12-20. Then you'd need 4 weeks to taper the miles you cover, with those next 4 weeks looking something like: 18-14-4-event day.

If you've got the luxury of 6 months or more, hold your long week at a certain distance for 2 weeks before jumping up a level, or climb by 1 mile each week instead of 2.

Also, if you are interested in marathon walking, you will need to put more of an emphasis not only on the long walks, but also on threshold walks, with less of an emphasis on anaerobic capacity sessions for speed. In most cases, some speed play on an easy walk every couple of weeks will satisfy your physiological need for building speed and efficiency.

If you find your experience characteristics fit the novice category, but you would like to do a marathon, it would be best to spend 2 to 3 months simply building mileage and overall strength before embarking on a marathon plan to avoid injury.

If you want to complete a faster marathon, but don't have the fitness base in walking, plan to train for a longer time to gain more strength, speed, and endurance. That might mean a "practice" marathon one year that you can simply complete without falling apart, while actually aiming for your real goal the following year. Some marathons— Portland and Los Angeles, for example—actually have had divisions for walkers, while others—Hawaii and Anchorage, for example—are walker-friendly because they allow the course and its aid stations to be open long enough for walkers, even slower ones, to finish without being forced off the road onto the sidewalks.

Now that you've got all the ingredients to seriously train, you might find you're interested in racing, which can be one of the truly satisfying end products of all the diligent training you've done. You'll find out why in the next chapter.

CHAPTER 8

RACING TO PR, RACING TO WIN

Racing opportunities are available for all levels of walkers and all levels of goals. There are the typical weekend "fun runs/walks" or community-oriented marathons. There are also youth track meets where little ones as young as 6 and 7 race in walk divisions, local-level race walks for all abilities, novice and all-comer events, and elite national-class races and meets for the extremely serious. Finally, there are masters races and track meets for anyone 35 and older, among whom the attendance goals range from Olympic aspirations to simple travel and tourism.

Whatever your walking goal, racing can add a new dimension to your training. Some of you might be hungry for the extra challenge of a race, and you'll find the endorphins are addictive. Some of you might shrug and shy away, "Oh, no, I don't want to race," and return day after day to your own training walks. No matter what you imagine you want, remember this: Racing is motivating, fun, and incredibly social, whether you're only walking the distance with a friend, walking against the clock for another PR, or racing hard against other walkers in pursuit of a medal.

Even if you don't care to ever chase a medal, jumping into a race now and then can enliven your training routine. Suddenly you have a bunch of people around you and the adrenaline rush often carries you to a new PR. Races also help you set goals along the way, motivating you to keep at it on down days, because you know you want to enter XYZ Community Fun Race. So don't discount racing if you don't think you're that serious. See it instead as a fun change of pace and a way to meet new people.

For those of you with a competitive bug who are already convinced that racing is in your future, we'll explain the details and technicalities of race walking rules and judging procedures after we take a look at different types and lengths of races available.

TYPES AND LENGTHS OF RACES

A key to your success will be to avoid biting off more than you can chew your first few times out. Choose a distance that seems short so you can finish it strongly and feel good about yourself and your effort. Then gradually accept the challenge of longer distances if you're interested in taking the time to train to support longer events. As explained in the training section, races longer than 10 kilometers need a solid base of miles for strength and injury prevention, especially once you approach half marathons and marathons. Although races of all distances exist (usually 3 to 20 kilometers), the standard international distance for Olympic walks will change in 1999 to 20 kilometers for women (from 10 kilometers), and remain 20 and 50 kilometers for men. Note that the longest footrace in the Olympic Games is the 50-kilometer men's race walk. At 31 miles it is nearly 5 miles farther than the marathon run of 26.2 miles!

Masters outdoor championships in the summer commonly have both 5- and 10-kilometer races for women, and both 5- and 20-kilometer races for men. Masters indoor championships in the winter offer a 3-kilometer distance. Youth meets slate 1,500-meter races for the youngest, then progress to 3-kilometer events, while older teenage girls at junior meets might do a 5-kilometer race and teenage boys have a 10-kilometer race.

Although in the United States the English system of miles is most common, you can see you'll need to begin to understand the metric system, since most races are measured in kilometers. See table 8.1 for a list of common race distances and their equivalents in miles.

To convert miles into kilometers, multiply the number of miles by 1.61 to get the number of kilometers. For example,

$$3 \text{ miles} \times 1.61 = 4.83 \text{ kilometers}$$

Table 8.1 Common Race Distances in Kilometers and Their Equivalents in Miles

Kilometers	Miles
2	1.24
3	1.86
5	3.1
8	4.96
10	6.2
12	7.44
15	9.3
20	12.4
30	18.6
40	24.8
50	31

To convert kilometers into miles, multiply the number of kilometers by .62 to get the number of miles. For example,

5 kilometers × .62 = 3.1 miles

Although this conversion from miles to kilometers or vice versa sounds confusing at first, you'll soon get used to the lingo as you hang around races and racers. Many race courses will still have mile markers, however, so you can clock yourself by the more accustomed mile and its increments.

WEEKEND FUN RUNS/WALKS

These community festivals are usually fund-raisers for some charity and offer a social way to get a workout, earn a T-shirt, and sometimes get some complimentary food and drink afterward. Don't be fooled, though, by organizers labeling one distance a "run" and another (usually the shorter one) a "walk." Anyone can run or walk either one. The only caveat if you choose to walk the longer distance (usually 10 kilometers, with a 2-mile or 5-kilometer shorter event) is that roads closed to automobile traffic for the runners often reopen after a set time, say 75 to 90 minutes. So if you can't complete the distance by

then, you'll have to retreat to the sidewalks to finish the distance and might not have water stations available or course monitors to show you the way as you finish.

You should also remember the following:

- Unless an organizer has a course "certified" (with a certification number provided), its distance may only be approximate. If you want exact measurements, before you enter ask about certification by, for example, USA Track & Field (USATF), the sport's national governing body, or the Road Runners' Club of America (RRCA).

- The shorter "walk" portions of these events often aren't timed, so if you want a finish time, ask about clocks.

- Mile markers might not be supplied on the shorter distances. If you want to know how you're progressing, ask whether "mile splits" are offered. Some larger races have volunteers standing at each split calling out the running time as participants pass by.

- Race directors of events in most cities usually don't give prizes in the shorter "walk" divisions, nor do they award walkers in the longer distances. So you'll have to be satisfied with your T-shirt, a great workout, and the personal gratification of completing the event and beating some runners.

In most cities, these weekend events are not officially sanctioned and judged as race walks. That means you can walk them for fast training and a good workout, but if you're still learning race walking technique, you won't have any way to know if you were legal.

Some cities do have race walking divisions in these weekend events, with awards that are nearly comparable to the running divisions (for example, Indianapolis, Indiana; Albuquerque, New Mexico; and Denver, Colorado). However, these divisions are often only "monitored" for blatant cheaters—someone who literally jogs and doesn't even try to walk—rather than judged with a finely tuned eye, so your times still won't count for anything except personal satisfaction and a race-day award.

Many cities have free magazines that list area events; these are often found at technical running stores. Entry forms will give the details of awards, lengths of races, divisions and course, starting times, and contact numbers.

One bit of etiquette in these races: Slower runners and walkers should line up toward the back of the pack at the starting line. Leave the front section for those who will do their best roadrunner imitations. It's simply dangerous to both parties for a walker, especially one with a baby stroller or a dog on a leash, to be in front of these people. If you know you'll be doing 12-minute miles or slower, be smart, be kind, and stick to the rear.

JUDGED RACE WALKING EVENTS

Since these types of events are not commonly listed in local athletic magazines and schedules, you have to be plugged in to the local race walking network to find out details. Check appendix B for resources for you to follow up on to find information in your area.

Although formally judged events, these can still offer a walker of any speed or ability a chance to test his or her technique in front of real judges, as well as to be timed and monitored by officials. Having judges eyeing your style doesn't mean you still can't have fun or that you have to be national class and able to do an 8-minute mile or less.

All levels participate in one field—especially since these events are often quite small compared to weekend runs where "small" means several hundred. In many local and regional race walks, you might have only 10 to 40 people with a mix that includes Olympians and novices. That mix is one reason that race walking is one big family. Everybody around the country gets to know each other, usually without class divisions based on rank. You might even find yourself on a starting line with an Olympian or national champion! Now, that won't usually happen in a running event.

No matter what level, walkers in search of a legitimate race should seek the following:

- An all-weather track or a certified course. If on a road loop—for example, 1 1/2 or 2K—you'll walk the same loop repeatedly until you reach the race distance.
- Judging by certified or experienced race walking officials, with at least four judges on a track and six judges on a road loop.
- Timing by several clocks and stopwatches to cover the possibility of failure by one.
- Monitoring by lap counters who record how many laps or loops a competitor has done to be certain of accurate race finishes.
- Separate men's and women's events on a track when the event is up to and including 10 kilometers, if records might be set or qualifying times for a championship are to be valid. Road races may be mixed.
- Bib numbers to be pinned to the front of a competitor's shirt. Championship races will supply a double set of numbers—one for your back too—so judges will be able to identify you once you've passed them.
- An introduction by the chief judge at the starting line, sometimes with race or course instructions.
- A separate person who is not competing in the event who will formally start the race.
- Officials who mandate that anyone who's disqualified leave the course and remove his or her bib number so as not to confuse judges or other competitors.

This seems like a foreboding list of requirements for formal events, but it's not any more complicated than the maze of officials and penalties in tennis matches or football games. In fact, having rules to follow and technique to practice is what makes racing more challenging, both mentally and physically.

RACE WALKING RULES

Rules are what keep race walking distinctively different from running and keep those technically untrained or those willing to cheat from destroying the event.

What many people don't realize is that competitive walking events have been an international tradition since the 1800s, with walking races circling England and other countries and attracting throngs of onlookers. Race walking of one distance or another for men has been an Olympic event since 1908, although women race walkers weren't accepted into the Olympic family of medal events until 1992, with competitors going faster and faster each year.

I'm not the only race walker who has been asked, "If you want to go fast, why don't you just run?" Well, I offer, if the only goal in life was getting somewhere the fastest, then hurdle races wouldn't exist, nor would the steeplechase, or even three-legged sack races! Race walking is a different event with different rules that allow those not following the rules to be disqualified, just as runners who step on a lane line can be disqualified or long jumpers who push off past the allowable mark can be penalized. It might look a little unusual to the untrained eye, but so does triple jumping or hurdling, both events that also require distinctive technique. The challenge of race walking is following the rules as well as getting somewhere faster than another contestant.

The rules, as written in the USA Track & Field rule book, are simple, and are still judged solely by the human eye:

> Race walking is a progression of steps so taken that the walker makes contact with the ground so that no visible (to the human eye) loss of contact occurs. The advancing leg must be straightened (i.e., not bent at the knee) from the moment of first contact with the ground until in the vertical upright position. (Paragraph VI, Rule 150, Page 108, USATF rule book)

Put more simply, formal race walkers must keep one foot on the ground at all times (figure 8.1), and they must keep the knee straight from the time the foot lands until it passes underneath the body, as judged by the human eye.

In slang terms, coming off the ground is called "lifting" (figure 8.1), and walking with bent knees is called "creeping" (figure 3.17).

Figure 8.1 Lifting the knee or pushing the arms too high can cause walkers to lift themselves off the ground known formally as *loss of contact*.
Adapted from USATF.

RACE WALKING JUDGING

Judging is not a matter for a novice, since it takes a finely trained eye to catch the minute differences between lifting and not, or bending a knee and not, especially when you have to watch several walkers zipping past you all at once at moderate to high speeds. In most areas of the country, judges must take training courses, pass tests, and participate in apprenticeship programs so others may review their ability before they receive entry-level certification.

Entire training manuals and a video are available from USA Track & Field that explain the rules in detail and offer tips on matters as diverse as what to look for, where to stand, duties of different judges, how to fill out disqualification warning cards, and how to be professional and courteous in dealing with competitors.

As a competitor in a judged race walk, this is what you will experience First, once you're called to the starting line, the chief judge for that day's race will introduce him- or herself. He or she might also introduce the other judges, although that's not required.

Then, the chief judge and race director will explain very briefly in standard terminology—which you will get to know after a couple of races—the race's format, specifics about the course, and an overview of the rules (especially for any beginners in the field). At championship races details of rules will be dropped, since it'll be assumed competitors who have gotten that far know what to do.

He or she will also show the "judging paddles," "red cards," and "red paddle" and show where the "disqualification (DQ) board" will be posted, if there is one. Judging paddles (figure 8.2) look like table tennis paddles that have been painted white. On one side is a wavy line (representing loss of contact) and on the other side is an obtuse angle (representing a bent knee). After this short introduction, the chief judge will then step aside to a good position to view walkers at the start of the race. A starter will begin the event.

During the race is when the paddles, red cards, and DQ boards might be brought into action. If a judge thinks you are in danger of "lifting," or not achieving contact with both feet, he or she will make haste to your side as you pass, show you the side of the paddle with the wavy line representing loss of contact and say something like, "Number 33, caution for loss of contact" If he or she thinks you are in

Figure 8.2 Take the caution paddles as a technique tip.

danger of not achieving a straightened knee, the same thing will happen except you'll see the side of the paddle with the >-angle representing a bent knee.

You should acknowledge the judge with a nod or other gesture so the judge knows you have seen the paddle. You may receive one caution for each of the two violations from each judge, meaning if there are four judges on a track, you could see the paddle eight times if you aren't precise about your technique.

Remember two things, though: A caution only means that the judge thinks you are "in danger" of a violation, not that you actually have violated a rule. You may receive one or two white paddles from every judge and it will not affect your race finish. In fact, cautions are not unusual for top-level competitors and could mean only that they are pushing the technique envelope to attain maximum performance. Also, a caution shouldn't frighten you, make you stop, or otherwise lose concentration. Just nod and keep going.

A warning is an entirely different matter. That is the next step up from a caution, and three warnings mean you will be pulled from the field. If a judge thinks you have actually violated a rule, he or she will fill out a red card (figure 8.3) with the time of day and the violation he

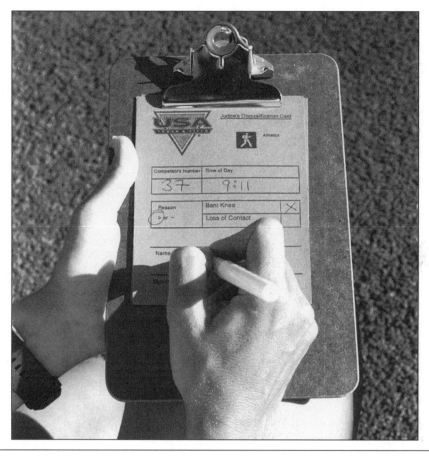

Figure 8.3 These cards—red in reality—will be filled out by a judge who determines a walker is not following the rules.

or she has noted, and pass it to a "DQ runner"—someone on a bike or on foot—who carries it to the race recorder. The race recorder does just that, records your violation on a form.

The recorder also works the disqualification board (figure 8.4), which is in sight of passing racers at the side of the course. On that board—not yet required equipment in local or regional races—he or she places a red dot or other mark beside a racer's bib number for the first two warnings/red cards.

Once you have three red cards, the chief judge (and only the chief judge) will step to your side and show you the red paddle, which is simply a red version of the white caution paddle, and say something like, "Number 33, you have been disqualified. Please step off the course and remove your number." Note that if you receive a third

Figure 8.4 Some races will have a disqualification board at the sidelines so racers can keep track of their progress.

warning, as a courtesy the red dot or X will not be placed on the board until after you've been notified by the head judge.

In figure 8.5, the racer would be safe from a red card because of maintained contact (a) and a straight knee (b). In (c), however, the racer would likely rack up a red card for loss of contact, while in (d) the red card would be for a bent knee.

Note that the rules do not require that you receive a caution before you earn a warning. If you are in violation of the rules as in (c) and (d) of figure 8.5, a judge could simply write you up and pass along the red card to the recorder. Also, once disqualified, you must leave the course or track. You can't just keep going, as beginners often want to do, just to see what your time would have been. Since your technique was deemed illegal, your time doesn't count either, and as a disqualified racer on the course you might lead legal walkers astray.

If you have begun to receive cautions in an event and you're worried about being disqualified, keep an eye open for DQ board postings. If you see one or two red marks appearing next to your number, it's time to be extra astute about your technique. Remember, receiving one or two red cards, but not a third that disqualifies you, means nothing. To say you were "almost disqualified" would be like saying you're a little bit pregnant. Either you are, or you aren't. Nevertheless, receiving red cards does mean you ought to return to technique training and find out if you've developed a bad habit. In some cases, you might want to politely approach a judge who might be willing to offer you some advice about what it was that he or she saw that caused the problem.

I vividly remember the first time I received a white paddle caution for loss of contact as a novice racer. After the race I was completely disarmed and worried, until a more experienced walker reached his hand toward me as if to shake hands. I took it. He indeed shook it and said, "Congratulations, you have now joined the elite because you are strong enough to be in danger of loss of contact." That was a real turning point, and allowed me to view cautions and warnings in a different light. They are truly an education about your technique and ability.

As a race walking competitor, you should be aware of three places that are danger spots for rule violations and that judges are trained to watch most closely: starting, passing, and finishing. In all three, a competitor has a certain amount of adrenaline and might let the moment get the best of him or her. Another danger at any time is a loss of concentration that might allow your technique to lapse. Competitors have received red cards in races for falling exhausted across the finish line in one final collapse that includes either a bent knee or a hop off the ground or both. If they're lucky, that will be only their first or second; if they are less fortunate, that ill-thought-out final moment could mean a third red card and a disqualification. Take heed as a beginner: No matter how tired you are, two more steps of maintained technique are always manageable. Look past the finish line, rather than at it, and save yourself a potentially grave mistake.

One note about trying to judge other race walkers: Because of the biomechanics of walking, it is next to impossible to judge other walkers in front of you or who are passing you. You might believe that a fellow competitor who passed you is "running," but unless you can stand to the side and watch the person from the proper judging position, any perception you have is likely incorrect.

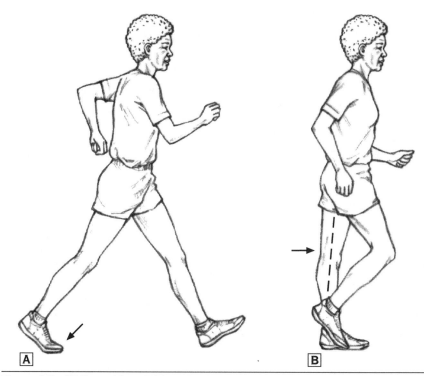

Figure 8.5 Walkers (a) and (b) in the illustration have achieved both contact and an extended knee, while walker (c) has lost ground contact and walker (d) has a bent knee, both violations that could earn the walker red cards.
Adapted from USATF.

PREPARING FOR RACING

Racing takes a certain toll on mind and body, which requires you to properly prepare for days or weeks ahead of the event. That means paying extra attention to cutting back on your training, getting enough rest, eating the right foods, and drinking enough fluids.

TAPERING

Tapering before a race or event in which you want to perform your best requires rest so you can "peak," which means allowing your body to reach its highest potential. This is what happens during Developmental Phase V. The term "rest" might be misleading, however, because although you will cut down on your mileage and training substantially, you will continue to work out nearly every day to keep your muscle memory and physical efficiency fresh and sharp.

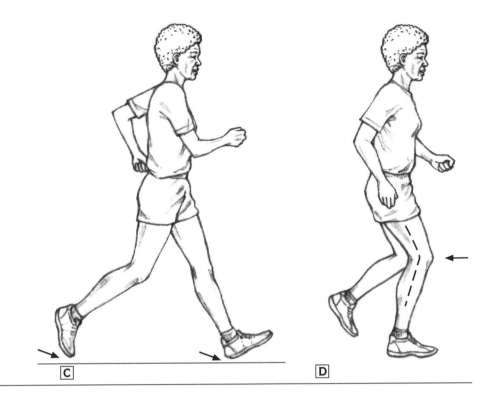

Combining appropriate rest with appropriate workouts allows your body to increase its anaerobic threshold as well as to replenish its stored glycogen, which is the fuel you'll use to power you during the event.

Studies show that not doing anything as a taper may increase your stored fuel but does nothing for your anaerobic threshold, while continuing to train as hard as usual in the 2 weeks prior to an important event lowers your fuel supply and maintains a tired cardiovascular system. Tapering only a few days helps somewhat—and this is appropriate before an event which you are using as training and for which you aren't entirely peaking—while tapering a week or so brings significant gains not only in your stored glycogen, but also in your anaerobic threshold.

Since a proper taper can require nearly 2 weeks of declining workouts and affects the training continuum that builds muscle strength and aerobic power, it's not to your benefit to taper for every event. Rather, choose no more than two, perhaps three, races each year and save your best effort for them.

© Lea Gallardo

For a successful taper, you will want to pay attention not only to its duration, but also to its volume, frequency, and intensity:

- **Duration**—As discussed previously, 7 to 10 days for up to a 10-kilometer event has been shown to provide the most replenishment of glycogen, highest gains in threshold, and best rest without loss of fitness or staleness. (Half marathons might need closer to a 14-day taper.)

- **Volume**—Drop your mileage in a stepwise fashion, slowly cutting back your typical volume by 50% to 70%. For example, if you normally walk 30 miles a week, you'll end up in your last week before an event walking only 10 to 15 miles.

- **Frequency**—Reduce training frequency by no more than 20%, meaning you will walk nearly the same number of days per week, only each workout will be much shorter. If you normally work out 5 days per week, you will walk no fewer than 4 days and perhaps still 5.

- **Intensity**—Despite a drop in mileage, intensity does not drop. The percentage of mileage that you do at a higher intensity will remain the same. For example, if at 30 miles you do 3 miles (10%) of aerobic capacity and 1 mile (3%) of anaerobic capacity workouts, once you hit 10 miles, you'll do about 1 mile of aerobic capacity workouts and perhaps a half mile or less of anaerobic capacity. That means each day will be short and sweet with a few quick intervals, leaving you with the feeling that you haven't worked out hard enough.

That's exactly the point of a taper—you should feel as if you can do more. You should feel light and well rested, so your body can stockpile energy reserves for your event.

Although this book has not focused on longer distance walking, note that marathoners need a slightly different schedule, since their training has taken them up to 18- or 20-mile long workouts that might last 4 or more hours, compared to others who reach a maximum long workout of 90 to 120 minutes. With 4 or more hours of fatigue buildup, marathoners need to begin their taper 3 to 4 weeks ahead of the event to allow more recovery. If you train for a marathon you should do no more than about a 3-hour walk 3 weeks before the event, then taper to about 90 to 120 minutes, dropping to 45 to 60 minutes the week before to finish recovery and increase stored glycogen. The same guidelines regarding gradually decreasing volume while maintaining frequency and intensity still apply.

SAMPLE TAPER FOR SPORT TRAINING

This sample assumes that you have in the last phase prior to the taper been working out approximately 20 to 25 miles a week, although you might have reached higher mileage earlier in the macrocycle. Most of these workouts have been unstructured based on minutes spent at a particular intensity and perceived exertion or heart rate, not on timing specific distances. This taper will cover the needed distance, but is therefore also based on time, not exact measured distances, and may be done on any trail or road.

Warm up and cool down for each workout with easy walking, 10 minutes each. Approximately 75% of the mileage in the taper is in the first 7 of the 10 days, with the remainder in the last 3 days before the event. Note that if you are following Novice Training and wish to taper before an event, you might prefer to follow this type of less formal

Sample Taper—Sport Training

Day	Workout
1	EZ 50 min
2	AC (5%) 2 × 5 min Equal rest of EZ walking
3	EZ 40 min
4	Rest
5	EZ 30 min
6	AnC (3%) 6 × 45 s Rest 2 1/2 min of EZ walking
7	Rest
8	AnC (2%) 6 × 30 s Rest 2 min of EZ walking
9	Rest
10	EZ with fartlek: 25 min with 2–3 sprints of 30–40 s each
	Event Day

system using time, rather than the more structured sample taper for race training. Percentages, as usual, are calculated based on total mileage, but here that refers strictly to the period of the taper.

SAMPLE TAPER FOR RACE TRAINING

This sample assumes that you have in the last phase prior to the taper been working out approximately 30 to 35 miles a week, although having perhaps walked more miles earlier in the macrocycle. Many of those workouts have been more formal and on tracks using exact distances and exact timing. This taper, therefore, is an example of using a track for most of your workouts.

Warm up and cool down for each workout with easy walking, 1 mile each. Approximately 75% of the mileage in the taper is in the first 7 of the 10 days, with the remainder in the last 3 days before the race. Note that if you are following Sport Training, you might prefer to use this kind of more formal taper instead of the sample sport taper based on time and intensity. Percentages, as usual, are calculated based on total mileage, but here that refers strictly to the period of the taper.

NUTRITION FOR PERFORMANCE

Eating the right foods can also make or break your taper and the successful event outcome it is trying to foster. For an event that lasts an hour or less, the old theory of carbohydrate loading is physiologically unnecessary, but that doesn't mean you can get away with feeding yourself platefuls of fat and sugar, either. A good athletic diet always includes 60%–70% carbohydrate, 20%–30% fat, and 10% to 20% protein. And there's no reason to veer from that before your event, especially since you need to stoke up your storage of glycogen, most of which will come from the carbohydrate. That doesn't have to be pasta. It can be foods such as baked potatoes or bread, too.

There are two important reasons—aside from trying to increase glycogen stores—to stick to good grains, pastas, and breads during your taper: One, they are easier to digest than fat or large quantities of protein and won't weigh you down when you want to feel light and ready to pounce. Two, they are comforting to the anxious precompetition soul. Some competitors swear by chicken noodle soup the night before a race. Now that's comfort food.

For longer events, especially those reaching 90 to 120 minutes and beyond, it's vital to top off your fuel tanks as high as they'll go to avoid "hitting the wall," a painful scenario where the world feels as if it's moving in slow motion and your legs and body feel heavy and sluggish,

Sample Taper—Race Training

Day	Workout	Mileage
1	AC (6%) 3 × 800 m Equal rest of EZ walking	4 mi
2	EZ	3 mi
3	AnC (4%) 2 × (300, 200, 100) Equal rest of EZ walking	3.25 mi
4	Rest	
5	EZ	3 mi
6	AnC (2%) 4 × 200 m Double rest of EZ walking	3.25 mi
7	EZ	2 mi
8	AnC (2%) 2 × (200, 100, 100) Double rest of EZ walking	2.5 mi
9	Rest	
10	2.5 mi with fartlek: 2–3 sprints of 30–40 s each at race pace	2.5 mi
	Event Day	

literally as if you've slammed into a brick wall. To me, it feels as if someone has poured my legs full of cement. This might be a sign you haven't pre-loaded well enough, or that you haven't had enough sustained carbohydrate intake during the event to keep you fueled. The wall will come for most people by about 90 minutes, with more fit and highly trained athletes able to go longer—perhaps 120 minutes or so. Preparing for events of those durations means pumping up your carbohydrate intake as high as 80% of your diet for a few days before the race.

As for fluids, dehydration can be a racer's biggest foe. So drink plenty of fluids for a couple of days before. Never allow yourself to feel thirsty. Carry a water bottle with you wherever you go. You should have to urinate about every hour or so, and your urine should be nearly clear. Try to avoid salty foods or too much caffeine, which will counteract your good intentions by drying you out more.

See appendix A for reference to good sports nutrition resources.

PREPARING YOUR MIND

Following a plan to prepare yourself physically for an event is the easy part. Making sure your mind is ready for the jitters, anxiety, and self-doubts is an entirely different matter.

Don't for a moment think that you, as a racing novice, are the only one playing these mental tag games with yourself. Athletes of all ages and abilities suffer from the pangs of competitive nerves, and many top-level athletes have seen a sport psychologist to help them work through personal doubts or competition fears. Sport psychology is a skilled profession that combines the best of psychological therapy with a knowledge of the needs and pressures that surface in athletic situations. At the highest levels of competition, the mind can make the difference between a gold medal and an also-ran. At other levels, your mind can mean the difference between a successful race and a frustrating experience.

It would be impossible—and even insulting to the sport psychology profession—to try to summarize ways to train the mind for competition in a couple of pages. For that, there are entire books. We'll just look briefly at a few key points of mental training.

Find Your Ideal State of Arousal

Sport psychologists know that any good performance must include a certain level of stress. If you aren't psyched up enough, performance will likely be low; if you're revved up too much, performance will also be low. The key is finding the place on the curve, illustrated in figure 8.6, that's optimal for you.

For most people, that will take some experimentation during workouts. For example, many people get too nervous and excited, so if you are one of those, you should try to take a few moments before a workout while standing or sitting with your eyes closed, breathing deeply, relaxing your shoulders, and seeking a momentary oasis of calm in your gut. Take yourself away from the anxiety of the workout or race ahead and spend a moment floating in that oasis while allowing your body to relax. Try imagining a large glowing ball in your center that slowly spreads its peaceful waves of energy to the tips of your fingers and the toes of your feet. Begin to feel your whole body tingling in the same way you might feel just before you fall asleep. After just a few minutes, open your eyes and tackle the workout, trying to keep the centered, energized, yet peaceful feeling you found in the oasis moments before. For those who need extra psyching up, you can jump and scream and listen to rock 'n roll.

Take Teeny Bites, Not One Gulp

Races can seem dauntingly long. "I'm going to walk how far? 12 miles? I can't do that," your mind tells your body. Your body responds by tensing and your mind starts to freeze. The best way around this is to

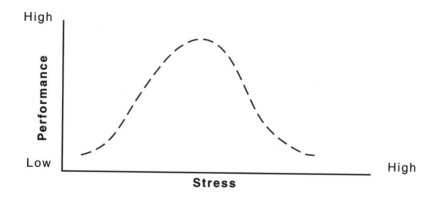

Figure 8.6 Performance arousal curve. Many sport psychologists believe performance tends to increase as stress increases, but only to an individually optimal point, before more stress causes performance to decrease.

trick yourself into small bites. It's not a 6-mile race. It's six 1-mile races. It's not 2 miles, but only eight quarter miles. Even in workouts, baby steps work. Avoid telling yourself during a 12-mile workout that you still have 8 miles to go. Rather, tell yourself that you've already done 4. Remember, the glass is half full, not half empty. Paint the picture the way it feels best to you. During 10-kilometer races on a track, it's deadly to think of all 25 laps. Instead, you focus on the lap you're on, finish it, then focus on the next lap. In reality, you're completing twenty-five 400-meter races.

FOCUS ON THE PROCESS, NOT THE OUTCOME

One of the more difficult tasks for many, including myself, has been to focus not on the time I want to accomplish, but on the process of getting there. Sport psychologist Dr. Betty Wenz, who has worked with various teams and athletes for several decades, helped me learn the difference. As a competitor, you'll need to stay in the moment by simply checking in with your body, making sure you feel OK, staying relaxed, and keeping an eye on split times (your times along the way, such as each quarter mile or mile). One of the best races I ever had was one where I never even thought about what my final time would be, but simply put myself in a machine-like zone where I ticked off each lap on the track of a 10-kilometer race within a second or so of the mile pace I wanted to accomplish. I'll never forget the excitement of going into my last lap and finally looking at the cumulative time on my watch. Then, and only then, did I realize I was going to have a hefty PR.

VISUALIZE SUCCESS

Sport psychology research has discovered that frequently spending a few minutes visualizing your event and imagining yourself doing well and feeling good can act to transfer those feelings to the actual event.

Sit or lie down comfortably, close your eyes, and imagine yourself at the event, preferably at the site where it will be if you are familiar with it. Start with your warm-up and take yourself step by step through to the finish. The point is to allow yourself to experience in your mental rehearsal positive and successful feelings that will ingrain themselves in your mind and become a part of you the day of the event, supplanting any anxieties or stress.

A good sport psychology book can describe the process of mental rehearsal, as well as other mental training techniques that can help you through an event.

One caution about mental side effects of a taper: Most likely, as a dedicated exerciser, you will feel antsy, unsettled, and as if you're losing your fitness. Know that those emotions aren't unusual. For example, a 1996 study showed that even 3 days of exercise deprivation in regular exercisers caused mood disturbances, anxiety, depression, and tension (Mondin, 1996). Also know that doing a few extra workouts or doing a few at a slightly higher intensity will only give you a momentary psychological and physiological boost, while they'll set back the rest your body needs to perform at its best for the upcoming event.

Find other ways to distract yourself and enjoy the extra free time to relax or to employ the mental techniques described here.

Now that you have all the technique and workout advice, training programs, and racing information, one last invaluable step is knowing how to monitor yourself by keeping a training log, which can also help you stay motivated to keep on walking.

CHAPTER 9

KEEPING TRACK AND STAYING MOTIVATED

Better walkers are also diligent writers. That is, keeping a detailed logbook of your training helps you reach your goal for many reasons.

For one, you have a black-and-white record of concrete data such as distance covered, time it took, and paces you've walked. That can help you realize the progress you're making toward your goal because it's easy to forget what you did a month ago, let alone a year ago. With a training log, you can refer to past workouts, compare them to current entries, and give yourself a pat on the back—even after workouts you might call bad.

You can also use the data to keep yourself on track and motivated. It might be easy to shrug off a needed workout now and then, but suddenly when you have to write down a big zero on that day and those big zeros start adding up, you'll be more motivated to get back at it. If there's a particular reason for the lapse, such as sick kids or business travel, write that down too. You could discover a pattern that will need some thoughtful methods of intervention.

In addition, you can get to know your body better. Tired spells might turn out to be a harbinger of impending illness. Restless sleep or depressions could indicate something in life that needs changing. Working out with a certain person might push you a little harder, but then workouts for the next 3 days are particularly difficult—perhaps an indication that person pushes too hard for you. Writing down such vital signs teaches you how to tune in and, even more importantly, how to listen.

Last, your log can act as a personal coach, telling you through the physiological and behavioral data you've recorded when to pick up the pace or add more mileage, and when you might need a rest or a few easy workouts. Patterns can also help you eventually establish, for example, what time of day results in better workouts, whether sleep shortfalls affect a workout, or if certain foods the night before a workout cause discomfort or sluggishness.

As you can see, time and distance are central aspects of any logbook, but they are not the most revealing part. You need to keep track of other aspects of training, including emotional state, feelings, sleep, and appetite, because they can shed light on the subtleties of how workouts are affecting you and how you are progressing toward your goals.

WHAT TO LOG

The basics fall into four categories. But that doesn't mean you can't jot down under general comments anything that suits your fancy and might help you along the way. See figure 9.1 for a sample of a logbook page.

PHYSIOLOGICAL DATA

This section should include the mechanics of the workout. Record the type of workout (for example, long or anaerobic threshold); your goal for the day in distance, pace per mile, heart rate intensity, or RPE (or any combination of these four variables); what you actually accomplished in distance and intensity; your heart rate ranges or averages (depending on whether you own a heart rate monitor and which model it is), and your recovery heart rate.

I've found that having my goal in the same place in the notebook as what I did helps me put into perspective days or months later whether I was on track or not for where I wanted to be in my training. I also like to note both pace per mile and heart rate range. If, for example, my pace was slower than expected but my heart rate was on target, I can assume I was particularly tired, mentally unfocused, or something in the air bothered my allergies. If the heart rate is still in the appropriate range, the workout can nevertheless in most cases be called successful because it still fulfilled the physiologic goal for that day.

Recovery rates, say at 1 or 2 minutes after you're done or between intervals, are some of the best gauges of fitness level. You'll get to know exactly where your pulse should be within 2 minutes after a race or hard workout. If it's not there, you'll know there's something askew with your body.

ENVIRONMENTAL DATA

Note the location of your workout, time of day, temperature, wind, perhaps even humidity and smog levels. Don't forget to note the terrain of your workout location, such as rough spots or hills, that could affect the overall time. Crowds or even toddlers darting across a track can also affect what you accomplish and your mental focus.

The weather, for example if you had a headwind on the last 6 miles of a long workout or a headwind on the back 200 meters of each lap of a threshold workout on the track, is an extremely important part of a workout to log. Each person's sensitivity varies, but you'll probably come to recognize if factors such as low or high humidity or smog play havoc with your workout.

More than anything, this section will help you establish patterns that you can use in your favor in a quest for successful workouts, locations, and times.

PSYCHOLOGICAL/BEHAVIORAL DATA

Did you have fun? Was the workout a grind? Make a note about your mental state and ability to focus that day. Another important contributing factor could be whether you had enough sleep the night before. Sometimes recording what your mood was before a workout compared to after a workout can be enlightening, too.

Describe these elements with more than vague words such as "kind of tired." Try finding ways to rate the fun, fatigue, or focus, such as on a scale of 1 to 5. That'll make it easier to compare one workout to the next. Use the "Comments" section for such information.

CROSS-TRAINING ACTIVITIES

Log what else you did, such as weightlifting, stretching, or abdominal exercises. If you didn't walk, note what else you did do, such as a

Day / Date_____

Workout type_____

Workout

    Goal_____

           _____

    Accomplished_____

    _____ Miles / Minutes_____

    HR / Intensity_____

Warmup ❑   Cooldown ❑   Stretch ❑

Location_____ Time of day_____

Weather / Conditions_____

_____

Comments_____

_____

_____

_____

_____

Other activities_____

_____

_____ Abdominals / Back ❑

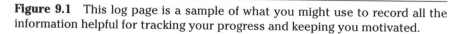

Figure 9.1   This log page is a sample of what you might use to record all the information helpful for tracking your progress and keeping you motivated.

workout on a stair climber or a meandering bike ride. Even a long day wandering through a street fair can be tiring and might affect your energy level the next day, so note other efforts or simply time spent on your feet.

MISCELLANEOUS TIPS

Under the "Comments" section, jot down anything you desire. For example, any aches or soreness, new shoes or clothes, chafing that irritated you, a friend who talked too much, or whether you had to rush the workout or cut it short because of an appointment.

OVERALL SUMMARIES

At the end of each week, tally up your mileage or total workout time, and any other items that might help you, such as average resting heart rates. If you're trying to lose weight, you might note your body weight and if your clothes are fitting differently, indicating fat loss.

Once a year, include your cholesterol count, blood pressure reading, and body fat percentage. These are all important contributors toward overall good health of which you should be aware.

To record the information, you'll need a notebook with plenty of space. Don't try to crunch everything into a tiny square on a calendar or into a corner in your appointment book. I've found that I've become wordier over the years, taking the time to note distractions on the track or trail, somebody I stopped to talk to, or even distinctive smells that irked me.

Feel free to develop your own shorthand, pictures, symbols, or abbreviations for items you note. Try using mathematical symbols, such as < or =. Develop your individual way of ranking workouts in terms of meeting your day's goals, such as plus and minus signs, or even smiley and frowny faces. If you're bilingual, experiment with foreign words that are shorter than their English counterparts. Be creative and use what you'll understand. No one else needs to decipher the scrawl.

Make it easy on yourself to record the information promptly by keeping your logbook in your car, on your desk, in your briefcase, or anyplace where you'll see it and keep up-to-date entries.

MOTIVATION TIPS

The logbook, as I said, can be one tool in keeping you motivated. Just the process of writing down information, knowing you'll write down data, and having the pages staring back at you can keep you on the path toward your goal.

But there are other ways to stave off the boredom monster.

VARY YOUR WORKOUTS

Mix up your walks. That's one reason choosing from a varied menu each week helps you stay excited. Obviously, different types of workouts serve different developmental goals, but even within each type there is a broad selection of possibilities. Use your imagination. Come up with alternatives based on the descriptions outlined. Then each workout, each week, and each cycle will be different and something to look forward to.

CHOOSE DIFFERENT LOCATIONS

You'll go stir crazy if you go to the same place day in and day out. Make an effort to go to different neighborhoods, tracks, or trails so each day seems fresh. If you must go to the same place, who says you have to start at the same point on a trail? Start at a different end. Who says you have to go right, then circle back? Go left instead. Who says you have to go all the way out, then turn around? Go halfway, loop back, then do it again. Zoos, gardens, older neighborhoods with architecturally historic homes, and even malls can be great places to keep yourself entertained.

CHALLENGE YOURSELF

Try a workout that seems a little daunting, or walk with a friend who might go faster. You'll never know if you don't try. You have to be willing to fall on your face a few times in the course of discovering your potential. As part of your training, participate just for fun in local noncompetitive volksmarches or walkathons.

OPEN YOUR EYES

Every trail and neighborhood has its idiosyncrasies. Notice leaves changing colors, people in the windows, tenants coming and going, baby birds on a pond, a new fence, or a fresh coat of paint. Avoid a monotonous tromp with glazed eyes fixed straight ahead. You should be able to describe what's along your route and even tell stories about the people you saw and what they were wearing!

CREATE CONTESTS

Either enter mileage contests sponsored by the President's Council on Physical Fitness and Sports or the American Running and Fitness Association, or create your own. For example, hang a regional map on a wall and move a pin each day after your walk to see how far you've traveled. Match your success with a friend—who can reach a certain city first?—then celebrate by taking each other to a movie or enjoying some other treat.

MEET NEW FRIENDS

If you go to one area often enough, you'll get to know the others out there when you are. Talk to them. Or even if you don't talk, say hello, wave, and smile. I have dozens of workout buddies, many of whom will ask where I've been if I was out of town. In most cases, we don't even

know each other's names, but we know when we're missing or doing something differently.

Sometimes one of my mystery trail buddies and I have ended up finishing about the same time, and I've struck up a conversation to find out more about them. Once you've seen someone for months or years, you can't help but wonder who that person is.

KEEP OLD FRIENDS

Create a network of walking buddies around your city and even around the country. From my experience, walkers are real people, usually very down-to-earth and sincere. Once you tap into the walking network, you'll be surprised how quickly it will develop into one big family. All you have to do is call a fellow walker in a neighboring state and say you're going to be in town, and that person will pick you up for local workouts if needed, suggest local routes and tracks, or tell you about area events.

You'll have friends in every nook of the country who will understand your love of walking, swap tales of training, share stories about mutual acquaintances, or keep you informed about happenings.

These days, some of my best friends are fellow walkers, people I've met at various races or in other cities. Time and time again we travel together, meet to swap tales, share a pasta dinner the night before a race, and sometimes socialize even without a race or carbo-feed in sight.

One of these buddies is past national champion race walker and national record holder Jonathan Matthews. He tells a story that highlights how we walkers are people who can understand each other well, but whose activity is often misunderstood by unknowledgeable onlookers who only see someone walking so fast they could be running, and with a form that appears awkward. Some people, especially some runners, think you aren't working hard because you're walking. It doesn't matter that you're walking a faster pace—5 to 9 miles per hour—than they can run. One year in the early '90s at the San Francisco Marathon, Matthews was in a pack of runners doing a sub-8-minute mile when one looked over at him, then turned to his running partner and said, "Wow, he's going as fast as we're running!" To which the other replied, "Yeah, but he's only walking."

None of us are "only" walking. We are all athletes. We are all in training. And we are proud of that.

Keep your feet moving, my friend.

Appendix A

References and Suggested Readings

Alter, M. 1990. *Sport stretch*. Champaign, IL: Human Kinetics.

American College of Sports Medicine. 1995. *ACSM's guidelines for exercise testing and prescription*. Philadelphia: Williams & Wilkins.

Borg, G. 1982. "Psychophysical bases of perceived exertion." *Medicine and Science in Sports and Exercise* 14: 377-381.

Brittenham, D., and G. Brittenham. 1997. *Stronger abs and back*. Champaign, IL: Human Kinetics.

Burke, E., ed. 1998. *Precision heart rate training*. Champaign, IL: Human Kinetics.

Cairns, M., R.G. Burdett, J.C. Pisciotta, and S.R. Simon. 1986. "A biomechanical analysis of the racewalking gait." *Medicine and Science in Sports and Exercise* 18: 446-453.

Cavagna, G.A., and P. Franzetti. 1981. "The mechanics of competition walking." *Journal of Physiology* 315: 243-251.

Clark, N. 1997. *Nancy Clark's sports nutrition guidebook*. 2nd ed. Champaign, IL: Human Kinetics.

Franklin, B.A., K.P. Kaimal, T.W. Moir, and H.K. Hellerstein. 1981. "Characteristics of national-class race walkers" 9:101-108.

Hagberg, J.M., and E.F. Coyle. 1984. "Physiologic comparison of competitive racewalking and running." *International Journal of Sports Medicine* 5: 74-77.

Hreljac, A. 1993. "Preferred and energetically optimal gait transition speeds in human locomotion." *Medicine and Science in Sports and Exercise* 25: 1158-1162.

Iknoian, T. 1995. *Fitness walking.* Champaign, IL: Human Kinetics.

Loehr, J. 1994. *The new toughness training for sport.* New York: Dutton.

Martin, D., and P. Coe. 1991. *Training distance runners.* Champaign, IL: Human Kinetics.

Menier, D.R., and L.G.C.E. Pugh. 1968. "The relation of oxygen intake and velocity of walking and running in competition walking." *Journal of Physiology* 197: 717-721.

Mondin, G.W., W.P. Morgan, P.N. Piering, A.J. Stegner, C.L. Stotesbery, M.R. Trine, and M. Wu. 1996. "Psychological consequences of exercise deprivation in habitual exercisers." *Medicine and Science in Sports and Exercise* 28: 1199-1203.

Noakes, T. 1991. *Lore of running.* Champaign, IL: Human Kinetics.

Pollock, M.L., C. Foster, D. Knapp, J.L. Rod, and D.H. Schmidt. 1987. "Effect of age and training on aerobic capacity and body composition of master athletes." *Journal of Applied Physiology* 62: 725-731.

Rudow, M. 1995. *Advanced race walking.* 5th Ed. Seattle: Technique Productions, 4831 NE 44th Street, Seattle, WA 98105.

Taylor, P., and D. Taylor, eds. 1988. *Conquering athletic injuries.* Champaign, IL: Human Kinetics.

Tribole, E. 1992. *Eating on the run.* 2nd ed. Champaign, IL: Human Kinetics.

USA Track & Field. 1996. *Race walk judging handbook.* Indianapolis: USATF.

USA Track & Field. 1997. *Competition rules.* Indianapolis: USATF.

Wilmore, J.H., and D.L. Costill. 1994. *Physiology of sport and exercise.* Champaign, IL: Human Kinetics.

World Association of Veteran Athletes. 1994. *Age-graded tables.* Eugene, OR: National Masters News.

Appendix B

Selected Sources of Walking Information

USA Track & Field

USATF is the national governing body of track and field, the sport that also includes race walking and long-distance running. Local associations hold events, as do clubs within each association. If you don't know where to find the name and telephone number of your local association, call the national office in Indianapolis and ask for a referral. Your local association can give you the name of the area race walking chairperson or contacts at local clubs. Contact: USATF, P.O. Box 120, Indianapolis, Indiana 46206. 317-261-0500.

Ohio Racewalker

Ohio Racewalker is a funky little homespun newsletter that's one of the ultimate sources of race walking news as well as some gossip. Once you start reading it, you know you've become a groupie because it's mostly line after line of race results in teeny point size with plenty of endearing typos by founder and race walker Jack Mortland. You'll also find a few letters, some opinions about national and international topics, and a calendar of races around the country with contacts (although some inaccuracies slip in). Contact: *Ohio Racewalker,* 3184 Summit St., Columbus, Ohio 43202.

NATIONAL MASTERS NEWS

This is a newspaper covering master athletes (35+) from all track and field events. It includes results, international news, training advice, schedule information, profiles, and photos. Also available from *National Masters News* are publications that list records, age-grading, rules, and rankings. Contact: *National Masters News,* P.O. Box 50098, Eugene, OR 97405. 503-343-7716.

WALKING MAGAZINE

Walking Magazine contains mostly news about fitness walking and general health, but some columns cover training advice and technique. You'll occasionally find profiles or short stories about race walking, as well as a list of select race walking events by region. Available on most newsstands or call 800-829-3340 (U.S. and Canada), or 904-446-6914 (foreign) for subscription information.

WORLD WIDE WEB SITES

Obviously, World Wide Web sites on the Internet change constantly. But, as of publication, you could try **http://www.racewalk.com**. At that site the Wellness Center lists telephone contacts and race schedules. There you will also find the official newsletter of the National Race Walk Committee of USA Track & Field. Also try USA Track and Field's web site, **http://www.usatf.org**, or a wonderful site for history, pictures, and information by the International Amateur Athletic Federation, **http://www.iaaf.org/sport/walking.html**. Try searching under "walk" or "race walk" for other resources, local clubs, your association, and other sites.

INTERNET RACE WALKING
LIST SERVER

You can also subscribe to the race walking list server on the Internet by sending "subscribe racewalk" in the body (not the subject line) of an e-mail message to **majordomo@reed.edu.** Here you'll find national and international chat and gossip about races and such, as well as postings of race results, shoe reviews, and training information. Some of what is posted is helpful and from knowledgeable sources, but be forewarned that some postings are not from such knowledgeable sources. Remember to use a fine filter with any information you receive through this, or any other Internet web site, unless you can verify the person's education, knowledge, and validity.

INDEX

Note: Page numbers followed by *t* indicate that the entry is found in a table on that page. Page numbers followed by *f* indicate that the entry is found in a figure on that page.

ABOUT THE AUTHOR

Therese Iknoian is an exercise physiologist and nationally published freelance writer specializing in fitness, sports, and health. In addition to being the author of *Fitness Walking,* Therese has written articles for such magazines as *Walking, Self, Women's Sports and Fitness, Parenting, Men's Health,* and *Vitality.* She is also a contributing editor for *Walking* magazine and *California City Sports* and is a member of the editorial board for the American College of Sports Medicine's *Health & Fitness Journal.*

As a master walking instructor, Therese has spent several years working with corporations, health clubs, independent walking clubs, and professional conferences all over the world. She developed the Nike Run Walk program, has worked with Rockport and Side 1 as a program consultant, and is a member of the Adidas Global Advisory Panel and the PowerBar Team Elite. Therese also belongs to Team Polar, a group that educates people about the importance of heart-rate monitoring for effective exercise.

Therese is a nationally ranked competitive race walker. In 1994, when she was ranked 24th in the United States by *Track & Field News,* she broke the world record for the indoor 3K for her age group. Therese still holds the national record for the outdoor 3K. In 1995, she placed 14th in the Race Walk World Cup national trials. She also has numerous gold and silver medals in national masters championships.

Therese completed her master of science degree in kinesiology with an emphasis in exercise physiology and sport nutrition. She is certified as a health/fitness instructor by the American College of Sports Medicine and is gold-certified by the American Council on Exercise as a group fitness instructor. She also is certified as a coach and official by USA Track & Field.

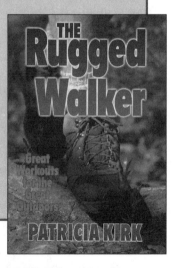

Books for complete fitness

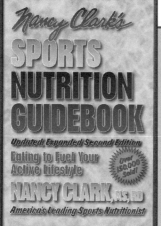